THINK AND GROW RICH

Dr. Maxwell Shimba

Printed by Shimba Publishing LLC
Printed in the United States of America

TABLE OF CONTENTS

INTRODUCTION

The Concept of Wealth

Wealth has always been a topic that stirs the imagination of people from all walks of life. But what is wealth, truly? For some, it is the tangible assets of money, property, and material possessions. For others, it is the freedom and security that wealth brings. Yet, the secret to wealth lies much deeper — in the intangible realms of the mind and spirit. This book aims to show you how wealth is more than a physical object; it is, at its core, an idea.

Understanding Money as an Idea

Money is often misunderstood as merely currency — paper notes, coins, or digital figures in a bank account. But in reality, money is much more than its physical form. It is a concept, an idea that represents value. At its core, money is a reflection of the value we create and exchange. It is not static but dynamic, and it flows to those who understand how to think about it correctly.

Think of money like a seed — small and full of potential. The way you nurture and grow that seed determines the abundance you will reap. The seeds of wealth are ideas, and by planting those ideas in fertile ground — your mind — you can create limitless prosperity.

Wealth begins as a thought, and thoughts become reality through focused intention, action, and belief. This is the foundational principle that this book will guide you through: Money is an idea inside of you. When you understand this, you begin to unlock the true potential of your mind to create wealth beyond what you can physically see.

The Power of Thought in Creating Wealth

What separates the wealthy from those who struggle financially is not luck, hard work, or even education — it is mindset. Wealthy individuals understand the power of thought. They realize that what they think shapes their reality, and they cultivate thoughts of abundance, success, and growth.

Thoughts are like magnets. They attract opportunities, people, and resources that are in alignment with them. By consciously thinking about wealth and abundance, you align yourself with the flow of prosperity. But merely thinking isn't enough. Your thoughts must be charged with belief, faith, and a burning desire to turn those thoughts into action.

The principle of thought leading to wealth is not new. Throughout history, the wealthiest and most successful individuals have tapped into this understanding. It's a universal law: What you think, you become. If you think rich, act rich, and believe in wealth, you will inevitably attract it into your life.

The Influence of King Solomon's Wisdom in Accumulating Wealth

King Solomon, one of the most revered figures in both religious and historical texts, stands as the epitome of wisdom and wealth. He was not only the wisest man who ever lived but also the richest. The secret to Solomon's wealth was not in the material treasures he possessed but in his profound understanding of the principles of wisdom and wealth.

When Solomon was asked by God what he wanted, he did not request riches, power, or fame. Instead, he asked for wisdom to govern his people well. In return for his selfless request, God gave Solomon not only wisdom but also unparalleled wealth. This story teaches us a critical lesson: True wealth is rooted in wisdom. When you have wisdom, the wealth naturally follows.

Solomon's life reveals a divine truth — wisdom brings wealth, and wisdom begins with the right mindset. By seeking wisdom and understanding the laws that govern wealth, you can unlock the same doors that made Solomon one of the richest individuals in history. His story exemplifies that the ultimate treasure is not money itself but the wisdom to generate and manage it effectively.

In this book, we will delve into the power of thought and wisdom in creating wealth. As we journey together, you will learn how to shift your mindset, nurture the seeds of wealth within you, and apply timeless principles to unlock abundance in every area of your life. Just as King Solomon understood that wealth is rooted in wisdom, you too will begin to understand that wealth is not just what you possess but what you believe and how you think.

Wealth is in Your Hands

You are the creator of your wealth. The thoughts you plant today will determine the harvest you reap tomorrow. Wealth is not a distant dream but a reality waiting for you to embrace it. By understanding money as an idea and harnessing the power of your thoughts, you will unlock the riches that have always been within you.

DR. MAXWELL SHIMBA

CHAPTER 01

THE POWER OF THOUGHT

The Mind as a Garden

Imagine your mind as a fertile garden. Just as a gardener carefully selects which seeds to plant in the soil, so too must you choose the thoughts and ideas that will take root in your mind. These thoughts are like seeds — they have the potential to grow and bear fruit, depending on how well you nurture them.

In the same way that a garden can grow beautiful flowers, fruits, or vegetables, your mind has the capacity to cultivate ideas that can lead to success, happiness, and wealth. However, the garden of your mind, like any other garden, requires attention and care. If neglected, it can become overrun with weeds — the negative thoughts and doubts that can choke out your potential for growth.

Planting the Right Seeds (Ideas)

Just as a gardener carefully chooses which seeds to plant, you must deliberately choose the thoughts and ideas that will take root in your mind. The seeds you plant are the foundation of what you will eventually reap in your life. If you plant seeds of abundance, success, and prosperity, you will grow a life rich in these qualities. On the other hand, if you plant seeds of doubt, fear, and negativity, your garden will reflect those thoughts.

Choosing the right seeds involves consciously directing your thoughts toward what you desire to achieve. Think of the wealth you want to build, the opportunities you wish to seize, and the success you aim to create. Plant these thoughts by focusing on them, visualizing your goals, and believing in the possibilities that lie ahead. Your thoughts are the first step in shaping the reality you want to live.

Nurturing Positive Thoughts About Wealth

Once the seeds are planted, the next crucial step is nurturing them. A gardener waters their plants, gives them sunlight, and protects them from harmful elements. In the same way, you must feed your positive thoughts with faith, focus, and action. Every day, nurture your thoughts about wealth by reminding yourself of your goals, visualizing your success, and reinforcing your belief in your ability to achieve financial abundance.

Nurturing positive thoughts also involves surrounding yourself with people, environments, and experiences that align with the wealth you wish to create. Just as a plant needs a healthy environment to thrive, your thoughts need the right conditions to grow. Stay in environments that inspire and uplift you, learn from those who have achieved financial success, and immerse yourself in knowledge that helps you grow.

The more you focus on nurturing positive thoughts about wealth, the stronger these thoughts become, until they eventually manifest in your life. Remember, just as a plant grows slowly over time, the process of building wealth through positive thinking is gradual but inevitable.

Removing Weeds (Negative Thoughts)

No garden is immune to weeds, and no mind is free from the occasional negative thought. Weeds in a garden are like negative thoughts — they compete for resources, take up space, and if left unchecked, can hinder the growth of healthy plants. In your mental garden, negative thoughts such as fear, doubt, and worry are the weeds that prevent your positive ideas from flourishing.

Removing these weeds is essential to maintaining a healthy mental environment for wealth creation. Whenever a negative thought arises, such as "I can't do this" or "I'm not good enough," recognize it for what it is — a weed trying to take root in your mind. Consciously pull it out by replacing it with a positive thought: "I am capable" or "I am on the path to success."

One of the most powerful ways to eliminate negative thoughts is through repetition of positive affirmations. These are statements that reaffirm your goals and abilities, such as "I am worthy of wealth," "I attract abundance," or "I have the power to create the life I desire." By regularly affirming these truths, you can prevent the weeds of doubt from overtaking your mind.

Weeds also come in the form of external influences. Negative people, toxic environments, and discouraging information can act as weeds that invade your mental garden. Be mindful of who and what you allow into your life. Protect your garden by surrounding yourself with positivity, encouragement, and inspiration.

Cultivating a Mindset for Success

Just as a garden requires constant care and attention to flourish, so too does your mind. The thoughts you choose to plant and the effort you put into nurturing them will determine the success and abundance you experience in life. By planting the right seeds, nurturing positive thoughts about wealth, and diligently removing the weeds of negativity, you can cultivate a mindset that attracts prosperity and growth.

Remember, your mind is a garden, and you are the gardener. The power to create a life of wealth and success is in your hands. With each positive thought, you are planting the seeds of a prosperous future.

Visualization and Belief

One of the most powerful tools in the journey toward wealth creation is the combination of visualization and belief. Together, these two forces form the foundation of every success story, allowing you to not only dream of financial prosperity but to actively create it.

The Importance of Believing in Your Ability to Create Wealth

Belief is the cornerstone of all achievement. Without belief in yourself and in your ability to create wealth, no amount of effort or planning will bear fruit. Belief acts as the internal fuel that keeps you moving forward, even when external circumstances seem discouraging. It gives you the confidence to pursue your financial goals with persistence and determination.

When you truly believe that you are capable of creating wealth, you open yourself up to opportunities that others may overlook. You begin to see the world through a lens of possibility and abundance. On the other hand, doubt and disbelief act as barriers, preventing you from recognizing the opportunities that could lead to financial success.

Believing in your ability to create wealth involves more than just wishing for it. It requires a deep-seated conviction that you are worthy of financial prosperity and that you have the skills, resources, and potential to achieve it. This belief must be unshakable, even in the face of challenges or setbacks. It is the belief that keeps you moving forward, knowing that wealth is not a distant dream but a reality you are actively creating.

To strengthen your belief, you must eliminate self-limiting thoughts and replace them with empowering ones. Whenever you encounter thoughts like "I can't do this" or "I'm not smart enough," remind yourself that these are not facts — they are beliefs that you have the power to change. By consciously choosing to believe in your ability to create wealth, you set the stage for success.

Visualizing Your Goals and Financial Success

Visualization is the act of mentally picturing the outcomes you desire, and it is one of the most effective techniques for achieving financial success. When you visualize your goals, you create a mental image of what you want your life to look like. This image becomes a blueprint for your actions, guiding you toward the realization of your dreams.

The process of visualization works because the mind cannot distinguish between real and vividly imagined experiences. When you consistently visualize yourself achieving your financial goals, your mind begins to act as if those goals are already within reach. You start to align your thoughts, decisions, and actions with the vision you hold in your mind.

To effectively visualize your financial success, follow these steps:

1. Be Specific: The more detailed your visualization, the more powerful it becomes. Instead of vaguely imagining wealth, picture yourself in specific situations of financial success. Visualize the amount of money you want to earn, the kind of lifestyle you want to live, and the steps you will take to achieve it. The clearer your vision, the more likely you are to manifest it.

2. Engage Your Senses: When visualizing your goals, engage all of your senses. Imagine what it feels like to achieve your financial success. Picture yourself living in the home of your dreams, driving the car you've always wanted, or helping others with your newfound wealth. By engaging your senses, you make your visualization more vivid and real to your mind.

3. Visualize Daily: Like any skill, visualization improves with practice. Make it a daily habit to spend time visualizing your financial goals. You can do this in the morning when you wake up or before you go to sleep. The more often you visualize, the more ingrained the vision

becomes in your subconscious mind, influencing your thoughts and actions throughout the day.

4. Feel the Emotions: Along with visualizing the external aspects of your success, focus on how it feels to achieve your goals. What emotions will you experience when you reach financial independence? Will you feel pride, relief, or joy? By connecting emotionally to your vision, you create a stronger bond between your present self and the future version of you who has already achieved success.

5. Take Action: Visualization alone is not enough; it must be paired with action. Once you have a clear mental picture of your financial success, take concrete steps toward making that vision a reality. Use your visualization as motivation to pursue opportunities, make strategic decisions, and persist in the face of obstacles. Visualization gives you the confidence to act as if your goals are already within reach.

Belief and Visualization: The Dynamic Duo

Belief and visualization are powerful individually, but together they create a dynamic force for wealth creation. When you believe in your ability to create wealth and visualize yourself achieving it, you align your mind, emotions, and actions with your goals. This alignment generates a momentum that attracts opportunities, people, and resources that bring your financial vision to life.

Belief without visualization can leave you without a clear direction, while visualization without belief can make your goals feel unattainable. But when you combine belief with vivid mental imagery, you create a pathway to success that is rooted in both faith and action.

In conclusion, the key to unlocking wealth lies within your mind. By believing in your ability to create wealth and consistently visualizing your financial success, you activate the law of attraction, setting in motion the forces that will bring your dreams into reality.

Visualization is the process of creating a vivid mental image of a desired outcome or goal. It involves using the mind to imagine what you want to achieve, with as much detail and clarity as possible. By mentally rehearsing the future you desire, visualization helps to shape your thoughts, emotions, and actions in ways that bring that vision into reality.

At its core, visualization taps into the power of the human mind's ability to transform thoughts into reality. The mind is an incredible tool that shapes our beliefs, actions, and ultimately, our experiences. When you visualize, you are essentially telling your brain what to focus on, what is possible, and what steps to take to achieve success.

The Importance of Visualization in the Power of Thoughts

Visualization is a critical aspect of the power of thoughts because it serves as a bridge between your ideas and your reality. Here's why visualization is so important when it comes to harnessing the power of your thoughts for success:

1. Creates Mental Clarity and Focus

Visualization forces you to clarify exactly what you want. Instead of having vague desires like "I want to be rich" or "I want to succeed," visualization requires you to define what success looks like. By visualizing specific goals, like a certain income level, a particular lifestyle, or a career achievement, you create a mental blueprint that guides your thoughts and actions.

This clarity of vision helps you stay focused. When your goals are vividly clear in your mind, you're less likely to be distracted by irrelevant tasks or discouraged by setbacks. Visualization helps to align your thoughts and energy toward the attainment of your goals, eliminating confusion and uncertainty.

2. Engages the Subconscious Mind

The subconscious mind is a powerful force that influences your decisions, behaviors, and beliefs. One of the most compelling reasons why visualization is effective is that it communicates directly with the subconscious mind. When you visualize your desired outcomes vividly, your subconscious mind accepts those images as reality.

The subconscious mind does not distinguish between a vividly imagined experience and a real one. By visualizing your goals as if they have already been achieved, you program your subconscious to work toward making that vision come true. This is why athletes often visualize their performance before competitions — their subconscious mind helps them perform better because it has already rehearsed success.

3. Strengthens Belief and Confidence

Visualization helps build confidence by allowing you to see yourself succeeding. When you consistently visualize achieving your goals, you start to believe in your ability to make them happen. Seeing yourself succeed in your mind's eye strengthens your self-belief and helps you overcome self-doubt and fear.

This confidence, in turn, translates into real-life actions. When you believe that your goals are attainable and that success is inevitable, you approach challenges with greater conviction and resilience. Visualization shifts your mindset from "Can I achieve this?" to "I will achieve this."

4. Enhances Motivation and Persistence

Visualization creates a deep emotional connection to your goals, which fuels your motivation. When you can see and feel the success in your mind, you become emotionally invested in achieving it. This emotional connection makes you more likely to stay motivated and persistent, even when obstacles arise.

By visualizing not only the end result but also the process, you prepare yourself mentally for the journey ahead. This preparation increases your perseverance because you've already seen yourself overcoming challenges in your mental rehearsal. When difficulties arise, you're more equipped to handle them because you've already visualized your success despite those challenges.

5. Aligns Thoughts with Action

Visualization is more than just daydreaming — it is a tool for aligning your thoughts with concrete actions. When you visualize your success, you are not simply imagining the end result; you are also mentally rehearsing the steps needed to get there. This mental rehearsal helps you take decisive, aligned actions in the real world.

For example, if you visualize achieving a financial goal, your mind begins to recognize opportunities, people, and resources that align with that vision. You become more aware of steps you can take to move closer to your goal. The clarity gained through visualization helps you prioritize your actions and make decisions that support your vision of success.

Visualization as the Key to Unlocking the Power of Thoughts

Visualization is the tool that brings your thoughts to life. It bridges the gap between the abstract world of ideas and the tangible world of results. By using visualization to see yourself achieving your goals, you train your mind to believe in the possibilities and to work toward them. It is the visual blueprint that guides your thoughts, actions, and emotions toward the success you desire.

CHAPTER 02

WISDOM AND WEALTH

Learning from King Solomon: Wisdom and Wealth

King Solomon, renowned for his wisdom, is one of the most prominent figures in history when it comes to the accumulation of wealth. His story, as recorded in the Bible, showcases how wisdom is intrinsically tied to the prosperity and abundance that many seek. Solomon's reign was marked by incredible wealth, influence, and success, and the root of his prosperity was not merely his position or power but the wisdom he received from God.

Solomon's story serves as an enduring example of how wisdom is a crucial foundation for wealth. It reminds us that financial success is not just about hard work or luck but about making thoughtful, informed decisions guided by deep understanding and insight. Let's explore how wisdom plays a critical role in wealth accumulation and how we can apply the wisdom of Solomon to modern financial decisions.

The Role of Wisdom in Wealth Accumulation

When Solomon became king, he was offered anything he desired by God. Rather than asking for riches, power, or a long life, Solomon asked for wisdom to govern his people effectively. Pleased with this selfless request, God not only granted him unparalleled wisdom but also gave him immense wealth, honor, and prosperity. Solomon's decision to prioritize wisdom over wealth illustrates a vital principle: wisdom is the foundation upon which lasting wealth is built.

Wisdom provides the clarity to make sound financial decisions, the foresight to invest in long-term success, and the discipline to manage resources wisely. Unlike riches that can come and go, wisdom endures and grows, providing the ability to continuously generate wealth.

1. Wise Decisions Lead to Lasting Prosperity: Solomon's wisdom enabled him to build a thriving economy and forge alliances that expanded his influence. Similarly, applying wisdom to financial decisions today means making choices that lead to sustainable prosperity rather than short-term gains. Wisdom helps us to weigh risks carefully, understand the value of patience, and avoid impulsive decisions that can lead to financial setbacks.

2. Insight Over Impulse: Wealth built on impulse, greed, or without a solid foundation of understanding is often fleeting. Wisdom, on the other hand, encourages the development of knowledge and insight before making any significant financial move. It calls for a comprehensive understanding of markets, investments, and the economy before diving in. Solomon's ability to discern the best course of action came from his wisdom, not from impulse or reckless ambition.

3. Wisdom Teaches the Value of Stewardship: Solomon's wisdom also made him a great steward of the resources he had. He knew how to manage wealth responsibly, allocate it for the benefit of his people, and maintain a flourishing kingdom. Wealth, when mishandled, can be lost quickly. However, wisdom instills the value of stewardship, teaching us to handle finances with care, invest wisely, and manage resources for future generations. A wise person understands that wealth is not just for personal gain but also for benefiting others and creating lasting impact.

Practical Applications of Solomon's Wisdom in Modern Financial Decisions

The wisdom of Solomon, though ancient, holds timeless lessons that can be applied to modern financial decision-making. Here are practical ways we can draw from Solomon's wisdom to build wealth today:

1. Seek Knowledge Before Making Financial Decisions

Solomon's wisdom was rooted in his thirst for knowledge and understanding. In today's fast-paced financial world, making uninformed decisions can lead to significant losses. Just as Solomon sought wisdom first, we should prioritize learning and understanding the financial landscape before making investments or taking on debt. Whether it's learning about stocks, real estate, business ventures, or financial markets, knowledge is the foundation of wise decision-making.

2. Invest for the Long Term

Solomon's wealth was built over time, through strategic partnerships and long-term planning. In the modern world, this translates into investments that grow steadily over time. Whether through long-term investments like retirement funds, real estate, or businesses that take time to mature, wise wealth accumulation is about planting seeds that will bear fruit in the future, not rushing for immediate returns.

3. Diversify Your Investments

Solomon diversified his wealth, investing in trade, alliances, agriculture, and construction. Today, this principle translates to diversification in your financial portfolio. Rather than putting all your resources into one area, spread your investments across different industries or asset classes. This minimizes risk and ensures that even if one area underperforms, your wealth continues to grow in other areas.

4. Seek Wise Counsel

Solomon's wisdom was so renowned that even leaders from other nations sought his counsel. We too must seek the advice of wise individuals when making major financial decisions. Whether through financial advisors, mentors, or experts in the field, having access to knowledgeable counsel can prevent costly mistakes and provide valuable insights.

5. Practice Patience and Delayed Gratification

One of the hallmarks of wisdom is patience. Solomon didn't rush into decisions or seek quick riches. He understood that wealth built over time is far more stable than wealth acquired quickly and without effort. In today's world of instant gratification, practicing patience and delaying gratification can be a game-changer. This means resisting the urge to spend impulsively or invest in "get-rich-quick" schemes and instead focusing on steady, long-term growth.

6. Use Wealth for a Greater Purpose

Solomon used his wealth not just for personal gain but for the betterment of his kingdom. He built the grand temple in Jerusalem, improved infrastructure, and made his people prosper. In our own financial journey, wisdom teaches us that wealth is not merely for self-indulgence. Using wealth to improve the lives of others, whether through charitable giving, investments that create jobs, or supporting causes you believe in, leads to fulfillment and lasting impact.

7. Protect What You've Built

Solomon's wisdom extended to protecting his wealth and kingdom through alliances and strong defenses. Similarly, wise individuals in today's world understand the importance of protecting their financial future. This might mean securing insurance, building an emergency fund, or creating legal structures like trusts to safeguard your assets.

Conclusion: Wisdom as the Key to Wealth

Learning from King Solomon, we see that wisdom is the ultimate key to wealth accumulation. Wealth built without wisdom is fragile and temporary, but wealth that is guided by wisdom endures and grows over time. By applying the principles of Solomon's wisdom in our financial lives — seeking knowledge, investing wisely, practicing patience, and using wealth for greater good — we can achieve sustainable financial success.

As you continue your journey to wealth creation, remember that true prosperity begins in the mind. Just as Solomon chose wisdom over riches and found that wealth naturally followed, when we choose wisdom in our financial decisions, wealth becomes the inevitable result.

Seeking Divine Guidance

Aligning Your Financial Goals with Higher Principles

In the pursuit of wealth and financial success, it's essential to remember that true prosperity begins with aligning your financial goals with higher principles. Wealth is not just about accumulating material possessions or achieving a certain status; it is about living in harmony with spiritual laws that guide and shape our existence. As believers, we are called to seek God's guidance in every area of our lives, including our finances.

The Bible teaches us that God desires to bless His people, but those blessings come when we align ourselves with His will. Proverbs 3:5-6 reminds us, "Trust in the LORD with all your heart and lean not on your own understanding; in all your ways submit to him, and he will make your paths straight." This passage highlights the importance of submitting our financial plans to God and trusting that He will guide us toward success when we seek His wisdom first.

When we make financial decisions with God's principles in mind, we ensure that our pursuit of wealth is not driven by greed or selfish ambition but by a desire to serve

His purposes. Matthew 6:33 further encourages this mindset: "But seek first his kingdom and his righteousness, and all these things will be given to you as well." In seeking divine guidance and prioritizing God's kingdom, we align our financial goals with higher principles, knowing that God will provide for all our needs.

1. Generosity and Stewardship: One of the key principles of biblical financial wisdom is generosity. Proverbs 11:25 states, "A generous person will prosper; whoever refreshes others will be refreshed." When we align our financial goals with God's principle of generosity, we open the door to blessings. Generosity not only reflects the heart of God, but it also positions us to receive greater financial abundance as we become stewards of His blessings to serve others.

2. Integrity and Honesty: Another crucial aspect of seeking divine guidance in our financial lives is the commitment to integrity. Proverbs 10:9 says, "Whoever walks in integrity walks securely, but whoever takes crooked paths will be found out." Aligning our financial goals with honesty and ethical conduct ensures that we are building wealth that is sustainable and pleasing to God. Wealth accumulated through dishonest means is fleeting, but wealth gained through righteous actions endures.

3. Contentment and Trust in God: Finally, seeking divine guidance in our finances means embracing contentment and trusting God's provision. Philippians 4:19 assures us, "And my God will meet all your needs according to the riches of his glory in Christ Jesus." When we trust in God's provision and remain content with what we have, we open ourselves to His divine provision without falling into the trap of materialism or greed.

The Relationship Between Spiritual Wisdom and Financial Prosperity

Spiritual wisdom plays a vital role in financial prosperity. True wealth is not just the accumulation of money or assets, but the ability to manage resources with discernment, discipline, and a heart aligned with God's will. The Bible offers numerous examples of how spiritual wisdom directly influences financial success.

1. Solomon's Request for Wisdom: The story of King Solomon is perhaps the most famous example of how spiritual wisdom leads to financial prosperity. When Solomon became king, he did not ask God for wealth or power. Instead, he asked for wisdom to govern his people effectively. As a result, God blessed Solomon with not only wisdom but also immense wealth. 1 Kings 3:12-13 records God's response: "I will give you a wise and discerning heart... Moreover, I will give you what you have not asked for—both wealth and

honor—so that in your lifetime you will have no equal among kings." This story illustrates that when we seek spiritual wisdom, financial prosperity often follows as a natural consequence of our alignment with God's principles.

2. Wisdom in Financial Stewardship: Proverbs 21:20 says, "The wise store up choice food and olive oil, but fools gulp theirs down." This verse emphasizes the importance of wise financial management. Those who use spiritual wisdom to steward their resources responsibly will experience financial security, while those who spend recklessly will face lack. Wisdom teaches us to save, invest, and manage our resources in a way that honors God and prepares us for the future.

3. Avoiding the Dangers of Wealth: While the Bible affirms that God blesses His people with financial prosperity, it also warns about the dangers of wealth. 1 Timothy 6:10 cautions, "For the love of money is a root of all kinds of evil. Some people, eager for money, have wandered from the faith and pierced themselves with many griefs." Spiritual wisdom helps us maintain a healthy relationship with money, ensuring that we do not fall into the trap of loving wealth more than we love God. It reminds us that money is a tool to be used for good, not an idol to be worshiped.

4. Humility and Gratitude: Spiritual wisdom also teaches us the importance of humility and gratitude in financial prosperity. Deuteronomy 8:18 reminds us, "But remember the LORD your God, for it is he who gives you the ability to produce wealth." Acknowledging that our ability to create wealth comes from God keeps us humble and grateful. It reminds us to use our financial resources for His purposes and to remain thankful for the blessings He has provided.

Aligning Wealth with Divine Wisdom

Seeking divine guidance in our financial goals leads to true and lasting wealth. When we align our financial plans with biblical principles—such as generosity, integrity, stewardship, and contentment—we position ourselves to receive God's blessings. Spiritual wisdom helps us to manage our resources wisely, avoid the pitfalls of greed, and use our wealth to make a positive impact on others.

As you move forward in your financial journey, remember that wisdom begins with the fear of the Lord (Proverbs 9:10). Trust in His guidance, seek His wisdom above all else, and watch how aligning your finances with His principles leads to both spiritual and financial prosperity.

CHAPTER 03

THE IDEA OF MONEY

Money, at its core, is not just paper bills, coins, or numbers in a bank account. It is a concept—a reflection of value that transcends its physical form. Money, as a medium of exchange, symbolizes the worth we attribute to goods, services, ideas, and labor. Understanding money as a concept shifts the way we approach wealth creation and financial success. It transforms our relationship with wealth from one of chasing material possessions to one of generating and managing value through the power of ideas.

In this chapter, we will explore how money is a reflection of value and how ideas are the seeds that generate wealth. As we delve into these concepts, we will draw wisdom from the Bible, particularly the teachings of King Solomon, whose insights on wealth and prosperity are timeless.

Money is a Reflection of Value

At its most fundamental level, money is simply a tool that reflects value. It allows us to exchange something of worth for goods or services. But the value behind money is not inherent in the money itself. A $100 bill, for example, only has value because society agrees that it does. The true worth lies in what the money represents—the value of the work done, the resources used, or the service provided.

King Solomon, in all his wisdom, recognized the importance of understanding value. Proverbs 13:11 says, "Wealth gained hastily will dwindle, but whoever gathers little by little will increase it." This verse teaches that the real value of wealth is not in getting money quickly, but in understanding the principles of steady, sustained accumulation of value. Solomon knew that wealth accumulated with wisdom and patience retains its value over time, whereas quick gains are often fleeting.

The Bible also speaks of the importance of integrity in creating value. Proverbs 22:1 states, "A good name is more desirable than great riches; to be esteemed is better than silver or gold." Here, we see that true value is not just in the accumulation of money but in the reputation and trustworthiness that underlie it. Money without value— whether moral, ethical, or practical—is ultimately worthless.

Therefore, we should seek to build wealth that reflects true, lasting value, rooted in integrity and wisdom.

How Ideas Generate Wealth

One of the most powerful forces behind wealth creation is the power of ideas. Ideas are the seeds from which wealth grows. Every great financial success, every profitable business, and every innovation began as an idea. The ability to think creatively and recognize opportunities for value creation is what separates those who accumulate wealth from those who remain stagnant.

The Bible, particularly in the teachings of Solomon, often links wisdom with the generation of wealth. Proverbs 8:12-18, where wisdom is personified, says, "I, wisdom, dwell together with prudence; I possess knowledge and discretion... With me are riches and honor, enduring wealth and prosperity." Wisdom, as Solomon describes, is the root of wealth because it gives birth to ideas that create value. By aligning ourselves with wisdom, we position ourselves to recognize and act upon opportunities that generate wealth.

Ideas are not limited by resources, background, or circumstances. They are boundless and available to everyone willing to seek them. King Solomon, in Ecclesiastes 11:4, encourages us not to be paralyzed by uncertainty or doubt: "Whoever watches the wind will not plant; whoever looks at the clouds will not reap." This teaches us that waiting for the perfect moment or fearing potential risks will prevent us from acting on ideas that could generate wealth. Wealth creation requires taking calculated risks, nurturing ideas, and trusting in the process.

Additionally, Proverbs 24:3-4 reinforces this principle: "By wisdom a house is built, and through understanding it is established; through knowledge its rooms are filled with rare and beautiful treasures." In this context, building wealth is likened to building a house. It starts with the idea, the blueprint, but it is wisdom, knowledge, and understanding that transform the idea into something tangible and valuable.

The Value of Vision and Planning

Just as ideas generate wealth, so too does having a clear vision and plan for how to execute those ideas. King Solomon was a master of strategic planning. Under his leadership, Israel flourished economically, culturally, and spiritually. Solomon's wealth was not just a product of chance but of careful planning and execution of his ideas.

In Proverbs 21:5, Solomon offers a key principle: "The plans of the diligent lead to profit as surely as haste leads to poverty." Diligence in planning and acting on ideas ensures that value is maximized, while rushing without proper thought often results in loss. Vision without action is useless, but a clear, well-executed plan transforms ideas into financial success.

Likewise, Proverbs 16:3 advises, "Commit to the Lord whatever you do, and He will establish your plans." This highlights the importance of aligning our financial goals with divine principles. When we commit our ideas and plans to God, seeking His guidance and wisdom, we position ourselves for success. Planning with spiritual insight and a strong moral foundation leads to not only material wealth but also a fulfilling and meaningful life.

Transforming Ideas into Action

While ideas are the seeds of wealth, they must be nurtured through action. An idea left idle has no power to create wealth. Solomon's wisdom shows us that wealth comes to those who act with diligence and perseverance. Ecclesiastes 9:10 encourages, "Whatever your hand finds to do, do it with all your might." This verse speaks to the necessity of putting effort and energy into your ideas if you want them to bear fruit.

It's easy to become overwhelmed by the magnitude of an idea, but Solomon teaches us that consistent effort over time leads to success. Proverbs 6:6-8 offers the example of the ant: "Go to the ant, you sluggard; consider its ways and be wise! It has no commander, no overseer or ruler, yet it stores its provisions in summer and gathers its food at harvest." This passage emphasizes the power of steady, disciplined work. Just as the ant works diligently to store provisions, so too must we diligently execute our ideas to generate wealth.

The Concept of Money and Ideas

Money, in its true essence, is a reflection of the value we create through our ideas, efforts, and actions. Solomon's wisdom teaches us that wealth is not gained through chance or luck but through the deliberate cultivation of ideas, guided by wisdom and aligned with higher principles. Understanding money as a concept and recognizing that ideas are the foundation of wealth empowers us to view financial success not as something distant and unattainable, but as something within our control.

As we continue this journey toward wealth creation, remember that it all begins with the power of a single idea. When nurtured with wisdom, guided by divine principles, and acted upon with diligence, that idea can blossom into lasting prosperity.

Turning Ideas into Wealth

Ideas are the seeds of wealth, but to transform them into tangible prosperity, one must learn how to identify the right ideas and develop the mindset required to bring them to fruition. Wealth creation is not just about luck or external opportunities; it's about recognizing potential in everyday situations and acting on them with an entrepreneurial spirit. In this chapter, we will explore how to identify profitable ideas and how to cultivate an entrepreneurial mindset that turns those ideas into wealth.

Identifying Profitable Ideas

Not every idea leads to financial success. The key to wealth creation lies in the ability to distinguish between ideas that hold potential and those that do not. Profitable ideas often solve a problem, fulfill a need, or create value in a way that is unique or better than existing solutions.

1. Look for Problems to Solve

Wealthy individuals are often those who solve problems. The bigger the problem, the greater the potential for wealth creation. Identifying gaps in the market or challenges people face on a daily basis is a great starting point for recognizing profitable ideas. Proverbs 14:23 states, "All hard work brings a profit, but mere talk leads only to poverty." This verse reminds us that effort and action are rewarded, particularly when directed toward solving real problems. By focusing on solving a need, you create value, and money naturally follows value.

2. Observe Trends and Innovations

Another way to identify profitable ideas is by observing current trends and innovations. The world is constantly changing, and with that change comes new opportunities. Paying attention to technological advancements, shifts in consumer behavior, or changes in the economy can help you spot ideas that have the potential to generate wealth. Ecclesiastes 3:1 reminds us, "To everything, there is a season, and a time for every purpose under the heaven." Recognizing the right time for a new idea is crucial for turning it into wealth.

3. Listen to Feedback

Sometimes, the best ideas come from the people around you. By listening to the needs, frustrations, and desires of your community, customers, or colleagues, you can uncover profitable ideas. Solomon's wisdom also teaches the value of listening to wise counsel and advice. Proverbs 15:22 says, "Plans fail for lack of counsel, but with many advisers they succeed." Seek feedback from others, ask questions, and pay attention to the ideas and needs expressed by those around you.

4. Be Willing to Innovate

The most profitable ideas are often those that bring something new to the table. Innovation is key to standing out in the marketplace. Don't be afraid to think outside the box or challenge conventional ways of doing things. Isaiah 43:19 says, "See, I am doing a new thing! Now it springs up; do you not perceive it?" This verse reminds us of the power of embracing new ideas and stepping into uncharted territory. Innovation often leads to breakthroughs that create new streams of wealth.

Developing an Entrepreneurial Mindset

Once you've identified a profitable idea, the next step is developing the mindset that will allow you to turn that idea into wealth. An entrepreneurial mindset is essential for anyone looking to succeed in the world of business or personal finance. This mindset encompasses creativity, resilience, and a focus on opportunities rather than obstacles.

1. Embrace Risk and Uncertainty

Entrepreneurship requires a willingness to take risks. While not every idea will succeed, those who are willing to step into uncertainty often find themselves rewarded. King Solomon understood the balance between risk and reward. Ecclesiastes 11:1-2 says, "Ship your grain across the sea; after many days you may receive a return. Invest in seven ventures, yes, in eight; you do not know what disaster may come upon the land." This passage speaks to the importance of diversifying and investing in opportunities, even when there's an element of uncertainty.

The entrepreneurial mindset is one that views risk not as something to fear but as a necessary part of the journey to success. Taking calculated risks is essential for turning ideas into wealth, and those risks are often the catalyst for breakthrough moments.

2. Persistence and Patience

Turning an idea into wealth takes time, and the path is often filled with challenges. Developing persistence and patience is key to long-term success. Many great ideas fail simply because the person behind them gave up too soon. Galatians 6:9 encourages us, "Let us not become weary in doing good, for at the proper time we will reap a harvest if we do not give up." In business, as in life, perseverance is the difference between success and failure.

Entrepreneurs understand that setbacks are part of the process and that every challenge is an opportunity to learn and grow. Patience is critical, as wealth creation is often a gradual process that requires consistent effort and determination over time.

3. Creativity and Adaptability

One of the hallmarks of an entrepreneurial mindset is creativity. Successful entrepreneurs think creatively about problems, solutions, and opportunities. They are not bound by traditional methods but instead seek new ways of doing things. Creativity allows you to differentiate yourself in a competitive market and to turn even ordinary ideas into extraordinary wealth.

Additionally, adaptability is a crucial trait for anyone pursuing entrepreneurial success. Markets change, and conditions shift. The ability to pivot and adapt to new circumstances can make the difference between failure and success. Proverbs 16:9 reminds us, "In their hearts humans plan their course, but the Lord establishes their steps." While planning is important, being flexible and open to change is equally essential.

4. Focus on Value Creation, Not Just Profit

An entrepreneurial mindset is driven by the desire to create value, not just to make a quick profit. When you focus on creating something that benefits others—whether it's a product, service, or solution—financial success naturally follows. Proverbs 11:24-25 illustrates this beautifully: "One person gives freely, yet gains even more; another withholds unduly, but comes to poverty. A generous person will prosper; whoever refreshes others will be refreshed." The more value you create for others, the more wealth you attract into your own life.

5. Stay Teachable and Humble

Successful entrepreneurs remain lifelong learners. They understand that there is always more to learn and are willing to seek wisdom from others. Proverbs 1:5 advises, "Let the wise listen and add to their learning, and let the discerning get guidance." A teachable spirit allows you to continuously improve, adapt, and grow in your entrepreneurial endeavors.

Humility also plays a significant role in maintaining an entrepreneurial mindset. Wealth and success can easily lead to arrogance, but humility keeps you grounded and open to feedback, correction, and learning. Staying humble helps you build strong relationships and partnerships, which are essential in business.

Transforming Ideas into Wealth

Turning ideas into wealth requires more than just creativity—it requires wisdom, persistence, and an entrepreneurial mindset. By identifying profitable ideas that solve real problems, staying adaptable, and focusing on creating value for others, you can transform your ideas into tangible financial success. As you embark on your entrepreneurial journey, remember the words of Proverbs 16:3: "Commit to the Lord whatever you do, and He will establish your plans." By aligning your efforts with divine guidance and applying the principles of entrepreneurship, you can achieve lasting wealth and prosperity.

CHAPTER 04

THE LAW OF ATTRACTION

Attracting Wealth through Mindset

The Law of Attraction is a powerful principle that suggests our thoughts and emotions have the ability to shape our reality. It posits that what we focus on, whether consciously or unconsciously, draws corresponding circumstances and experiences into our lives. In the context of wealth creation, the Law of Attraction teaches that by maintaining a mindset focused on abundance, success, and prosperity, we can attract financial opportunities and resources. This chapter explores how thoughts influence financial success and how gratitude plays a crucial role in attracting wealth.

How Your Thoughts Attract Financial Opportunities

The idea that your thoughts have a direct impact on your financial success is not merely theoretical; it is supported by both scientific research and spiritual teachings. The basic premise is that what we consistently think about influences our actions, decisions, and ultimately, the outcomes we experience. In the context of wealth, maintaining a positive, abundance-focused mindset helps align your thoughts and behaviors with opportunities for financial growth.

1. The Science Behind Thought and Action

The connection between thoughts and real-world outcomes is rooted in psychology and neuroscience. Cognitive Behavioral Therapy (CBT) is a well-established psychological framework that emphasizes how thoughts influence emotions and behaviors. By changing your thought patterns, you can change your actions and thus your results. This principle is similar to the Law of Attraction: if you consistently think about wealth and success, you're more likely to take actions that lead to financial opportunities.

In addition, neuroscience shows that our brains have a mechanism called the Reticular Activating System (RAS), which filters information and focuses on what is deemed important. When you focus your thoughts on financial success, your RAS prioritizes information and opportunities related to wealth, making it easier to spot and act upon them. This concept is not mystical but a scientifically proven function of the brain.

2. Biblical Evidence for the Power of Thought

The Bible also supports the idea that thoughts play a significant role in shaping reality. Proverbs 23:7 says, "For as he thinks in his heart, so is he." This verse reinforces the notion that our inner thoughts directly influence our outer reality. If we believe in scarcity, we will act in ways that perpetuate scarcity. Conversely, if we think thoughts of abundance, we will attract experiences and opportunities that align with prosperity.

Another example is found in Romans 12:2, which instructs us to, "Be transformed by the renewing of your mind." This transformation involves shifting your thoughts and perspective to align with divine principles, which in turn affects your actions and the outcomes you experience. By renewing your mindset to focus on abundance and wealth, you open the door to financial transformation.

3. The Placebo Effect: Belief Creates Reality

One of the most well-documented psychological phenomena that illustrates the power of thought is the placebo effect. This effect occurs when patients experience real improvements in health after receiving a treatment that has no therapeutic value, simply because they believe it will help them. The placebo effect demonstrates how deeply our thoughts and beliefs influence our physical and mental reality.

In the context of wealth creation, the placebo effect serves as evidence that what we believe can manifest in tangible outcomes. If you believe you are capable of attracting wealth, and consistently think and act in ways that support that belief, your external reality is likely to align with your internal conviction.

The Role of Gratitude in Attracting Abundance

Gratitude is a powerful emotional state that plays a critical role in the Law of Attraction. By expressing gratitude for what you already have, you create a positive emotional vibration that attracts more of the same into your life. Research shows that practicing gratitude has tangible effects on emotional well-being, which directly influences one's mindset and behavior toward wealth and success.

1. Scientific Evidence for Gratitude and Success

Studies in psychology have demonstrated that gratitude enhances well-being, reduces stress, and increases optimism—all of which contribute to better decision-making and a more proactive approach to life. A study published in the journal Personality and Individual Differences found that people who regularly practice gratitude experience higher levels of positive emotions, which contribute to success and satisfaction in life, including financial success.

Gratitude shifts your focus away from what you lack to what you already have, fostering an abundance mindset.

Dr. Robert Emmons, one of the leading researchers on gratitude, has shown that people who express gratitude regularly are more likely to achieve their goals, including financial ones. By focusing on what you have and being thankful for it, you set a positive tone that attracts more abundance into your life.

2. Gratitude in Scripture

The Bible emphasizes gratitude as an essential practice for attracting blessings and favor. Philippians 4:6-7 says, "Do not be anxious about anything, but in every situation, by prayer and petition, with thanksgiving, present your requests to God." The act of expressing gratitude, even before receiving what we desire, invites peace and opens the door for abundance. This principle is directly aligned with the Law of Attraction, as it teaches that when you are thankful for what you already have, you naturally attract more.

Additionally, 1 Thessalonians 5:18 instructs us to, "Give thanks in all circumstances; for this is God's will for you in Christ Jesus." Gratitude, therefore, is not just a practice but a divine mandate that positions us to receive more of God's blessings, including financial abundance.

3. Gratitude as an Emotional Amplifier

From the perspective of the Law of Attraction, emotions are powerful amplifiers of thought. When you combine positive thoughts about wealth with the emotional state of gratitude, you intensify your ability to attract financial opportunities. Gratitude helps you maintain a higher emotional vibration, which is essential for drawing abundance into your life. Proverbs 17:22 says, "A cheerful heart is good medicine, but a crushed spirit dries up the bones." This shows that maintaining a positive emotional state, such as gratitude, is not only good for your health but also for attracting wealth.

The Mindset for Attracting Wealth

The Law of Attraction teaches that your thoughts and emotions have a profound influence on your financial reality. By focusing on abundance, cultivating a positive mindset, and practicing gratitude, you can align yourself with the opportunities and resources that lead to wealth. This principle is supported by both scientific research and biblical teachings, proving that your mindset has the power to shape your financial future.

Whether you are just beginning your journey toward financial success or seeking to deepen your understanding of wealth creation, remember that your thoughts and emotions are your greatest tools. As you harness the power of positive thinking, belief, and gratitude, you will find that wealth is not just a distant goal but an attainable reality within your grasp. Proverbs 18:21 reminds us, "The tongue has the power of life and death, and those who love it will eat its fruit." In the same way, your thoughts have the power to create or destroy your financial destiny. Choose wisely, and watch as the Law of Attraction brings abundance into your life.

The Science Behind Attraction

The Law of Attraction is often described as a spiritual principle, but it also has roots in psychological science. The idea that our thoughts influence our reality is supported by both spiritual and scientific evidence. This chapter explores the psychological and spiritual principles behind the Law of Attraction and provides real-life examples of how positive thinking has led to wealth creation.

The Psychological Principles of the Law of Attraction

The Law of Attraction is based on the principle that like attracts like — what you think about consistently shapes your reality. From a psychological perspective, this idea is backed by well-established concepts in the fields of cognitive psychology and neuroscience.

1. The Power of the Subconscious Mind

One of the key psychological mechanisms behind the Law of Attraction is the power of the subconscious mind. The subconscious mind governs much of our behavior and decision-making, often without our conscious awareness. When we repeatedly focus on positive thoughts — such as financial success, wealth, and abundance — these thoughts begin to reprogram our subconscious mind. As a result, we start to act in ways that align with those thoughts.

The subconscious mind is incredibly powerful in filtering information. This process, known as selective attention, means that when we focus on a specific outcome (like financial success), our brain starts to filter out irrelevant information and focuses on opportunities related to that goal. The subconscious mind acts like a magnet, pulling us toward the actions, people, and circumstances that match our dominant thoughts.

Neuroscience supports this idea through the concept of neuroplasticity — the brain's ability to rewire itself based on repetitive thought patterns. Positive thinking creates new neural pathways that reinforce behaviors aligned with achieving wealth, making it easier to identify and seize opportunities that lead to financial success.

2. The Role of Cognitive Biases

Another psychological explanation for the Law of Attraction is rooted in cognitive biases. These are mental shortcuts our brain uses to process information. When we adopt a positive mindset toward wealth creation, our brain develops what's known as a confirmation bias — the tendency to look for information that supports our existing beliefs. If you believe that wealth and success are achievable, you are more likely to notice opportunities and take action on them.

Conversely, if you harbor negative beliefs about wealth (e.g., "I'll never be rich" or "Money is hard to come by"), your brain will focus on information that confirms these beliefs, and you may overlook opportunities. By intentionally focusing on positive thoughts about wealth, you can shift your cognitive biases to support financial success.

3. The Impact of Positive Thinking on Behavior

Psychology also tells us that thoughts and emotions directly influence behavior. Cognitive Behavioral Therapy (CBT), a widely practiced psychological approach, emphasizes the connection between thoughts, emotions, and actions. Positive thinking leads to positive emotions, which in turn lead to productive actions. When you think positively about wealth and financial success, you're more likely to engage in behaviors that support those goals — whether it's saving, investing, or seeking out new business opportunities.

Proverbs 23:7 reinforces this idea from a spiritual perspective: "For as he thinks in his heart, so is he." What we think shapes who we are, and this spiritual principle aligns closely with the psychological understanding that thoughts lead to actions, and actions lead to outcomes.

The Spiritual Principles of the Law of Attraction

While psychology provides a scientific basis for the Law of Attraction, spiritual principles play an equally significant role. Many spiritual traditions, including Christianity, emphasize the power of faith, belief, and positive thinking in shaping one's reality.

1. Faith and Belief

The Bible teaches that faith is a powerful force that can shape reality. Hebrews 11:1 defines faith as "the substance of things hoped for, the evidence of things not seen." This aligns with the Law of Attraction, which suggests that believing in something — even before it manifests — is key to making it a reality. When you have faith in your ability to achieve financial success, you are aligning your thoughts with that reality, which increases the likelihood of it coming to pass.

Matthew 21:22 reinforces this principle: "And whatever you ask in prayer, you will receive, if you have faith." By maintaining a positive belief in your financial goals and combining it with action, you are more likely to achieve them.

2. The Power of Words

The Bible also teaches that our words have creative power. Proverbs 18:21 says, "The tongue has the power of life and death, and those who love it will eat its fruit." This suggests that the words we speak — whether positive or negative — have a profound effect on our reality. The Law of

Attraction builds on this by emphasizing the importance of speaking positively about your financial situation. By speaking words of abundance and success, you reinforce the positive thoughts needed to attract wealth.

3. Gratitude and Abundance

Spiritual principles also emphasize the importance of gratitude in attracting abundance. 1 Thessalonians 5:18 encourages us to "Give thanks in all circumstances." Gratitude shifts your focus away from what you lack and toward what you already have, creating a mindset of abundance. By practicing gratitude regularly, you align yourself with the energy of abundance, which attracts more of the same into your life. This is a key tenet of the Law of Attraction: what you focus on expands.

Real-Life Examples of Wealth Creation through Positive Thinking

1. Oprah Winfrey

One of the most well-known advocates of the Law of Attraction is media mogul Oprah Winfrey. Oprah has often spoken about how positive thinking and visualizing success were integral to her journey from poverty to becoming one of the richest and most influential women in the world. She credits her success to maintaining a mindset of abundance and focusing on gratitude, even during her most challenging times.

2. Jim Carrey

Actor Jim Carrey is another example of someone who used the principles of the Law of Attraction to achieve wealth and success. In the early stages of his career, Carrey famously wrote himself a $10 million check for "acting services rendered" and dated it five years in the future. He visualized receiving that amount of money for his work. In 1994, just before the date on the check, Carrey landed a role in Dumb and Dumber, which earned him $10 million. Carrey's story illustrates how maintaining a positive vision of success can lead to extraordinary outcomes.

3. Sarah Blakely

The founder of Spanx, Sarah Blakely, built a billion-dollar empire starting with just $5,000. Blakely attributes much of her success to her mindset. She practiced positive thinking and visualized her success long before it became a reality. She also embraced failure as a learning opportunity, which allowed her to stay focused and resilient through the challenges of building her business.

The Science and Spirit of Wealth Creation

The Law of Attraction, whether viewed from a psychological or spiritual perspective, is a powerful force that can transform your financial life. By maintaining a positive mindset, focusing on abundance, and aligning your thoughts, words, and actions with your goals, you can attract financial opportunities and create wealth. Real-life examples from successful individuals show that positive thinking, visualization, and gratitude are not just abstract concepts but practical tools for achieving financial success.

As you continue your journey toward wealth creation, remember the words of Romans 12:2: "Be transformed by the renewing of your mind." By renewing your mindset and embracing the principles of the Law of Attraction, you can unlock the full potential of your thoughts to create the financial future you desire.

CHAPTER 05

FAITH AND FINANCIAL SUCCESS

The Power of Faith in Wealth Creation

Faith is a powerful force that has the potential to shape not only your spiritual life but also your financial success. Faith, when directed toward your financial goals, can provide the foundation for wealth creation. It's not simply about wishful thinking or blind optimism; rather, it's about cultivating an unwavering belief in your ability to achieve financial prosperity, even when circumstances seem difficult. Faith fuels action, empowers resilience, and transforms challenges into opportunities.

The Bible speaks extensively about the role of faith in every area of life, including wealth and prosperity. Hebrews 11:1 defines faith as "the substance of things hoped for, the evidence of things not seen." This means that faith is the ability to believe in something before it becomes a reality. In the context of wealth creation, faith is believing in your financial success, even before it materializes. It is the belief that, despite obstacles or setbacks, financial prosperity is achievable when you commit to your goals and trust the process.

Building Unwavering Belief in Your Financial Goals

At the heart of faith is belief. To create wealth through faith, you must first build an unshakable belief in your financial goals. This belief must be strong enough to withstand challenges, setbacks, and periods of uncertainty. Without unwavering belief, it is easy to lose sight of your goals when things become difficult.

1. Clarify Your Financial Goals

The first step to building faith in your financial success is to clearly define your goals. What does financial success look like for you? Is it a specific income level, a thriving business, financial independence, or the ability to give generously? Clarity is crucial because faith thrives when you have a clear target. Habakkuk 2:2 advises us, "Write the vision; make it plain on tablets, so he may run who reads it." When you write down your financial goals, you make them concrete, and they serve as a guide for your faith.

2. Meditate on God's Promises of Abundance

The Bible is filled with promises of God's provision and abundance. By meditating on these promises, you can strengthen your belief in the possibility of financial success. Deuteronomy 8:18 reminds us, "But remember the LORD your God, for it is He who gives you the ability to produce wealth." This verse highlights the divine source of our ability to create wealth. When you anchor your financial goals in faith, you acknowledge that God is your provider, and that He empowers you to achieve financial success.

Another powerful verse is Philippians 4:19, which says, "And my God will meet all your needs according to the riches of His glory in Christ Jesus." This promise assures us that, through faith, we can trust that our needs will be met and that we have access to God's abundance.

3. Visualize Your Success with Faith

Visualization is a practical tool for building faith. When you visualize your financial goals with conviction, you are engaging your mind and spirit in the process of creating wealth. Visualizing your success helps you to internalize the belief that your financial goals are achievable. Mark 11:24 encourages us, "Therefore I tell you, whatever you ask in prayer, believe that you have received it, and it will be yours." When you visualize with faith, you are acting as though your financial success is already a reality, which strengthens your belief and motivates action.

Overcoming Doubt and Fear

Even with strong faith, doubt and fear can creep in and hinder your progress toward financial success. Fear of failure, doubt about your abilities, or worry about the future can all create obstacles on your path to wealth. However, faith has the power to overcome these barriers.

1. Confront Doubt with Faith

Doubt is often the enemy of faith. It causes hesitation and uncertainty, which can prevent you from taking action toward your financial goals. The Bible teaches us to confront doubt with faith. James 1:6 says, "But when you ask, you must believe and not doubt, because the one who doubts is like a wave of the sea, blown and tossed by the wind." This verse encourages us to stand firm in our faith and avoid the instability that doubt creates.

One way to confront doubt is to remind yourself of past successes and victories. Reflect on times when you've achieved goals or overcome challenges, and remind yourself that you are capable of doing it again. Faith grows stronger when we look back on what we've accomplished and trust that future success is possible.

2. Replace Fear with Action

Fear can be paralyzing, especially when it comes to financial risks or decisions. However, faith encourages us to take bold action, even in the face of fear. 2 Timothy 1:7 says, "For God has not given us a spirit of fear, but of power and of love and of a sound mind." This verse reminds us that fear is not from God, and that we have been given the strength to overcome it.

The best way to combat fear is to take action. When you step out in faith and take practical steps toward your financial goals, you begin to diminish the power of fear. Whether it's starting a new business, making an investment, or pursuing a new opportunity, action builds momentum and reinforces your belief in your financial success.

3. Trust the Process

Faith requires patience and trust in the process. Wealth creation is not always an overnight achievement; it often involves seasons of growth, learning, and perseverance. Proverbs 3:5-6 reminds us to, "Trust in the Lord with all your heart and lean not on your own understanding; in all your ways submit to Him, and He will make your paths straight." This trust in God's plan is essential when pursuing financial success. Even when you encounter setbacks or challenges, faith allows you to trust that everything is working together for your good.

When doubt or fear arises, remind yourself of the bigger picture. Trust that your faith, combined with action and persistence, will ultimately lead you to financial prosperity.

The Power of Faith in Action

Faith is not passive; it requires action. James 2:17 says, "Faith by itself, if it is not accompanied by action, is dead." This principle applies to wealth creation. While faith provides the belief and motivation, it must be paired with practical steps to bring financial goals to fruition.

1. Set Clear Financial Goals and Plans

Faith in wealth creation starts with a clear plan. Setting measurable financial goals allows you to act with purpose and intention. Break down your larger financial goals into smaller, actionable steps, and commit to working toward them with faith. Whether it's saving, investing, or starting a new venture, consistent action builds momentum and reinforces your faith.

2. Persevere Through Challenges

Faith also empowers perseverance. The path to financial success is rarely straightforward, but faith gives you the resilience to keep going. Galatians 6:9 reminds us, "Let us not become weary in doing good, for at the proper time we will reap a harvest if we do not give up." Perseverance is key to wealth creation, and faith sustains you through the challenges, knowing that the rewards will come in due time.

3. Give Generously with Faith

Faith in financial success also includes the principle of giving. Luke 6:38 says, "Give, and it will be given to you. A good measure, pressed down, shaken together and running over, will be poured into your lap." Generosity is an act of faith that not only blesses others but also opens the door to greater abundance in your own life. Giving demonstrates trust in God's provision and invites His blessings into your financial journey.

Faith as the Foundation for Financial Success

Faith is the foundation for financial success. By building an unwavering belief in your financial goals, overcoming doubt and fear, and taking consistent action, you can harness the power of faith to create wealth. The Bible provides numerous examples of how faith leads to abundance, and these principles are as applicable today as they were in ancient times.

As you move forward in your financial journey, remember that faith is not just belief, but belief in action. Trust in your vision, align your goals with God's promises, and take bold steps toward achieving the financial success you desire. Faith will guide you, sustain you, and ultimately lead you to the wealth and prosperity that you seek.

Faith in Action

Faith in Action: Aligning Your Actions with Your Financial Beliefs

Faith is a powerful force that shapes your mindset, beliefs, and expectations about wealth, but it must be coupled with action to manifest real-world results. James 2:17 reminds us, "Faith by itself, if it is not accompanied by action, is dead." This principle is especially true in the realm of wealth creation. While faith forms the foundation of your financial beliefs, it is your actions that turn those beliefs into tangible outcomes.

Steps to Take to Align Your Actions with Your Financial Beliefs

To turn faith into financial success, you need to ensure that your actions reflect your beliefs. If you believe that wealth is possible for you and that financial success is part of God's plan for your life, your actions must be consistent with those beliefs. Here are key steps to align your actions with your faith-driven financial goals:

1. Set Specific Financial Goals

Faith begins with a clear vision of what you want to achieve. Without clear goals, your actions can become scattered, and your faith may lack direction. Setting specific, measurable financial goals is the first step in aligning your actions with your beliefs.

Proverbs 29:18 says, "Where there is no vision, the people perish." Without a clear financial vision, it is difficult to move forward with purpose. Start by writing down your financial goals—whether it's saving for a home, paying off debt, starting a business, or achieving financial independence. Be specific about what you want to achieve and the timeline you expect to accomplish it in. By setting clear goals, you give your faith a target to work toward and your actions a roadmap to follow.

2. Create a Financial Plan and Budget

Once your goals are defined, the next step is to create a financial plan that aligns with those goals. Faith-driven wealth creation is not about random or impulsive financial decisions. It's about taking deliberate, calculated steps that reflect your commitment to success.

A financial plan should include a budget, savings goals, and an investment strategy. By creating a budget, you ensure that your money is being used in ways that support your long-term financial objectives. Luke 14:28 emphasizes the importance of planning: "Suppose one of you wants to build a tower. Won't you first sit down and estimate the cost to see if you have enough money to complete it?" This verse teaches us the importance of financial preparation and strategic planning.

3. Take Consistent Action

Faith in action is about consistency. Small, daily actions taken toward your financial goals add up over time. Whether you're saving a portion of your income, investing in your future, or paying down debt, it's the regular, consistent steps that build momentum.

Proverbs 13:11 reminds us, "Dishonest money dwindles away, but whoever gathers money little by little makes it grow." This principle highlights the importance of gradual, steady progress in building wealth. Faith may inspire you to dream big, but it's the small, faithful steps that ultimately lead to success.

4. Invest in Your Education and Skills

Faith-driven financial success requires wisdom and knowledge. As you pursue your financial goals, continue to invest in yourself through education, learning new skills, and seeking financial wisdom. Proverbs 4:7 advises, "The beginning of wisdom is this: Get wisdom. Though it cost all you have, get understanding." Financial literacy is essential for wealth creation, and gaining knowledge helps you make informed decisions.

Whether you're learning about investing, managing money, or improving your skills in your career, personal growth directly impacts your financial success. Align your actions with your belief in your ability to grow and succeed by continually improving yourself.

5. Give Generously

Faith in action is not just about accumulating wealth for yourself but also about giving generously and using your resources to bless others. Proverbs 11:25 says, "A generous person will prosper; whoever refreshes others will be refreshed." Generosity is a key principle of faith-based wealth creation. By giving to others, you demonstrate trust in God's provision and sow seeds that bring further abundance into your life.

Make giving a regular part of your financial plan. Whether through charitable donations, tithing, or helping those in need, giving generously not only blesses others but also reinforces your belief that abundance flows to and through you.

Faith as the Foundation of Wealth-Building Strategies

Faith is not just an abstract belief; it is the very foundation upon which successful wealth-building strategies are built. Faith provides the mindset, vision, and resilience necessary for achieving financial success. Here's how faith underpins key wealth-building strategies:

1. Faith Fuels Long-Term Vision

One of the core aspects of faith is the ability to see beyond present circumstances and focus on future possibilities. Wealth-building is a long-term endeavor that requires the ability to stay focused on your goals despite temporary setbacks or challenges. Faith provides that long-term vision, allowing you to persevere through difficult times.

Hebrews 11:6 teaches, "And without faith it is impossible to please God, because anyone who comes to Him must believe that He exists and that He rewards those who earnestly seek Him." Faith reminds us that, with patience and diligence, our financial efforts will be rewarded in due time. A long-term vision is critical for investments, business growth, and building sustainable wealth.

2. Faith Encourages Risk-Taking

Building wealth often involves taking calculated risks, whether it's investing in the stock market, starting a new business, or pursuing new opportunities. Faith enables you to take these risks with confidence, trusting that God is guiding your steps and that success is possible even in uncertain situations.

Ecclesiastes 11:1 encourages risk-taking in faith: "Cast your bread upon the waters, for after many days you will find it again." Taking risks, when guided by wisdom and faith, is essential for growth. Faith allows you to trust in the process and believe that even in risky situations, opportunities for success will emerge.

3. Faith Builds Resilience

Setbacks are inevitable on the journey to wealth, but faith builds the resilience necessary to keep moving forward. Challenges such as financial losses, failed investments, or unexpected expenses can derail your progress if you lack faith. However, faith provides the inner strength to bounce back, learn from failures, and continue toward your goals.

James 1:3-4 speaks to the resilience that faith builds: "Because you know that the testing of your faith produces perseverance. Let perseverance finish its work so that you may be mature and complete, not lacking anything." Faith in action means trusting that every challenge is part of the journey and that perseverance leads to maturity and financial success.

4. Faith in Abundance, Not Scarcity

Wealth-building strategies based on faith operate from a mindset of abundance, not scarcity. Instead of focusing on what you lack, faith allows you to see the opportunities for growth, expansion, and success. Philippians 4:19 assures us, "And my God will meet all your needs according to the riches of His glory in Christ Jesus." With faith, you can confidently approach financial decisions knowing that there is enough for everyone and that your efforts will be met with God's provision.

Aligning Faith with Action for Financial Success

Faith without action is incomplete, but when combined, they create a powerful force for financial success. By setting clear goals, planning wisely, taking consistent action, and giving generously, you align your faith with the practical steps needed for wealth creation. Faith provides the foundation for long-term vision, risk-taking, resilience, and an abundance mindset, all of which are essential for building wealth.

As you continue your financial journey, let faith guide your actions. Trust that God's promises of abundance are true, and that your faith-driven efforts will bear fruit in due time. Proverbs 16:3 reminds us, "Commit to the LORD whatever you do, and He will establish your plans." When faith and action are aligned, financial success becomes not just a possibility, but a reality.

CHAPTER 06

GOAL SETTING AND PLANNING

Creating a Financial Blueprint

Wealth creation does not happen by chance; it requires intentionality, planning, and a clear vision of where you want to go. Just as an architect needs a blueprint to build a structure, you need a financial blueprint to build your wealth. Goal setting and planning are foundational steps in this process, allowing you to transform your financial dreams into actionable steps. In this chapter, we will explore how to set clear, measurable financial goals and develop a concrete plan to achieve them.

Setting Clear, Measurable Financial Goals

The first step to creating your financial blueprint is to set clear, specific, and measurable goals. Without clarity, it's easy to lose focus and become overwhelmed by the numerous financial possibilities and challenges. Well-defined goals provide you with direction, motivation, and a roadmap for success.

1. The Importance of Specificity

When setting financial goals, specificity is key. Vague goals like "I want to be rich" or "I want to save more money" are difficult to achieve because they lack focus. Instead, your goals should be specific, providing a clear target to aim for. Proverbs 21:5 emphasizes the importance of planning: "The plans of the diligent lead to profit as surely as haste leads to poverty." Diligent planning begins with specific goals that guide your actions.

For example, instead of saying "I want to save money," a specific goal would be "I want to save $10,000 over the next 12 months." By specifying the amount and timeframe, you create a clear objective that is easier to track and achieve.

2. Make Your Goals Measurable

Once you've set specific goals, make sure they are measurable. Measurable goals allow you to track your progress and adjust your actions if needed. A measurable goal answers questions like "How much?" and "By when?" For instance, if your goal is to pay off debt, a measurable version would be, "I want to pay off $5,000 of credit card debt by December 31."

Measurable goals keep you accountable and motivated, giving you a clear sense of accomplishment as you move closer to achieving them. Habakkuk 2:2 advises, "Write the vision; make it plain on tablets, so he may run who reads it." When your goals are clearly defined and measurable, they serve as a guiding vision that keeps you on track.

3. Set Attainable and Realistic Goals

While it's important to dream big, your financial goals should also be realistic and attainable based on your current situation. Setting goals that are too ambitious can lead to frustration and discouragement if they are not achievable within a reasonable timeframe. To build momentum, start with goals that stretch you but are still within reach.

For example, if you are currently earning $40,000 a year, setting a goal to become a millionaire in one year may not be realistic. However, setting a goal to increase your savings by 20% or invest in an income-generating asset within the next 12 months is more attainable. Luke 14:28 reminds us, "Suppose one of you wants to build a tower. Won't you first sit down and estimate the cost to see if you have enough money to complete it?" By setting realistic goals, you create a foundation for long-term success.

4. Set Time-Bound Goals

Every financial goal should have a clear deadline. Without a timeframe, goals can become open-ended, making it easy to procrastinate. By attaching a deadline to your goal, you create a sense of urgency and motivation to take action. Time-bound goals help you break down larger financial objectives into smaller, manageable steps.

For example, if your goal is to save for a down payment on a house, setting a specific timeframe (e.g., "I will save $20,000 for a down payment within the next 24 months") provides a clear timeline to follow. Ecclesiastes 3:1 reminds us, "There is a time for everything, and a season for every activity under the heavens." Setting deadlines helps ensure that your financial goals align with the appropriate timing and seasons in your life.

Developing a Plan to Achieve Those Goals

Once your goals are clearly defined, the next step is to create a detailed plan to achieve them. This financial plan serves as your blueprint for turning your goals into reality. Without a plan, even the most well-defined goals can remain unattainable. Here are the key components of developing an effective financial plan:

1. Break Down Goals into Actionable Steps

Large financial goals can often feel overwhelming, but by breaking them down into smaller, actionable steps, you make them more manageable. For example, if your goal is to save $10,000 in one year, you can break that down into monthly savings goals of $833.33. Breaking down goals into smaller steps makes the process feel less daunting and allows you to measure progress regularly.

Proverbs 16:9 says, "In their hearts humans plan their course, but the LORD establishes their steps." Planning your course involves creating a series of steps that, when followed consistently, lead to your financial destination. Each step should be clear, actionable, and time-bound to ensure progress.

2. Create a Budget That Supports Your Goals

A budget is a critical tool in any financial plan. Your budget serves as a practical guide to managing your income and expenses in a way that supports your goals. Start by tracking your current spending and identifying areas where you can cut back to allocate more money toward your goals.

For instance, if one of your goals is to pay off debt, your budget should prioritize debt payments while minimizing discretionary spending. A well-structured budget ensures that your financial actions are aligned with your long-term goals. Proverbs 21:20 emphasizes the importance of wise budgeting: "The wise store up choice food and olive oil, but fools gulp theirs down." A budget helps you store up resources for your future rather than spending impulsively.

3. Build an Emergency Fund

A key part of any financial plan is building an emergency fund. Unexpected expenses can arise at any time, and having a financial cushion ensures that you don't derail your long-term goals in the face of an emergency. Aim to save at least three to six months' worth of living expenses in an easily accessible account.

Proverbs 6:6-8 teaches us the value of preparation: "Go to the ant, you sluggard; consider its ways and be wise! It has no commander, no overseer or ruler, yet it stores its provisions in summer and gathers its food at harvest." Just as the ant prepares for the future, building an emergency fund helps you prepare for unexpected financial challenges.

4. Monitor and Adjust Your Plan

A financial plan is not static; it requires regular monitoring and adjustments. Life circumstances can change, and it's important to revisit your goals and plan periodically to ensure they still align with your priorities. For example, if you receive a raise at work or have a new financial obligation, you may need to adjust your budget or savings goals.

Regularly reviewing your progress allows you to celebrate milestones and make necessary course corrections. Proverbs 27:23 advises, "Be sure you know the condition of your flocks, give careful attention to your herds." This principle applies to your financial resources as well—staying aware of your financial situation helps you make informed decisions and stay on track.

5. Seek Wise Counsel

Finally, it's important to seek wise counsel when developing your financial plan. Whether through financial advisors, mentors, or trusted friends with experience in wealth-building, getting advice from others can help you avoid costly mistakes and gain new perspectives on achieving your goals.

Proverbs 15:22 says, "Plans fail for lack of counsel, but with many advisers they succeed." Surrounding yourself with knowledgeable individuals who can provide guidance and support will increase your chances of success in achieving your financial goals.

Planning for Financial Success

Creating a financial blueprint is essential for turning your goals into reality. By setting clear, measurable, and time-bound goals and developing a plan to achieve them, you lay the foundation for long-term financial success. Remember, wealth-building is a process that requires intentionality, discipline, and consistent action. With a well-structured plan in place, you can confidently pursue your financial goals, trusting that your diligence and faith will lead to success. Proverbs 16:3 reminds us, "Commit to the LORD whatever you do, and He will establish your plans." When your financial goals are aligned with divine wisdom and guided by faith, you can achieve lasting prosperity.

The Importance of Consistency

Staying Committed to Your Financial Plan

Achieving financial success is not about grand, one-time efforts but about consistent, deliberate actions over time. Consistency is the key to transforming a financial plan from a set of ideas into tangible results. It is easy to feel motivated at the beginning of your financial journey, but the real challenge lies in maintaining that commitment day after day, month after month, especially when obstacles arise.

Proverbs 13:11 says, "Wealth gained hastily will dwindle, but whoever gathers little by little will increase it." This verse speaks to the power of small, consistent actions in building wealth. It is not about overnight success, but about steady progress, achieved through discipline and commitment.

1. Developing the Habit of Financial Discipline

Consistency in following a financial plan requires developing habits that support long-term success. Habits are actions that, when repeated consistently over time, become automatic. Saving a portion of your income every month, regularly reviewing your budget, and investing consistently are all examples of habits that lead to wealth accumulation.

Galatians 6:9 encourages us to persevere: "Let us not become weary in doing good, for at the proper time we will reap a harvest if we do not give up." Even when it feels difficult to stick to your plan, know that your persistence will eventually lead to a harvest of financial success.

Start by identifying key financial behaviors that need to become habits. For example, if your goal is to save more, set up automatic transfers to a savings account each month. If your goal is to reduce debt, commit to making additional payments toward your balance on a regular schedule. The more consistent you are in these small actions, the more they will compound over time.

2. Maintaining Focus Despite Challenges

Financial setbacks and challenges are inevitable, but staying committed to your plan in the face of adversity is essential for long-term success. Whether it's an unexpected expense, a job loss, or a market downturn, maintaining your focus on your financial goals will help you navigate difficult times with resilience.

James 1:12 offers encouragement for staying strong during trials: "Blessed is the one who perseveres under trial because, having stood the test, that person will receive the crown of life that the Lord has promised to those who love him." The same principle applies to your financial journey. Challenges are a test of your commitment, and if you persevere, you will be rewarded with financial stability and success.

One practical way to maintain focus is by regularly revisiting your goals. When you are clear about why you are pursuing financial success, it becomes easier to stay motivated during tough times. Remind yourself of the long-term benefits of sticking to your plan, whether it's financial independence, freedom from debt, or the ability to provide for your family.

3. Celebrating Small Wins

One of the best ways to stay consistent is by celebrating small wins along the way. Large financial goals can take time to achieve, and it's easy to feel discouraged if you don't recognize the progress you're making. By acknowledging and celebrating each milestone, no matter how small, you create positive reinforcement that keeps you motivated.

For example, if your goal is to pay off $10,000 in debt, celebrate when you reach the first $1,000. If your goal is to save for a down payment on a home, acknowledge your progress every time you hit a new savings milestone. Nehemiah 8:10 encourages us to find joy in our journey: "Do not grieve, for the joy of the LORD is your strength." Celebrating small victories provides the joy and encouragement needed to keep moving forward.

Adjusting Your Plan as Necessary Without Losing Sight of Your Goals

While consistency is crucial, it's also important to recognize that flexibility is sometimes necessary. Life is full of unexpected changes, and your financial plan may need to be adjusted as your circumstances evolve. However, adjusting your plan doesn't mean abandoning your goals. The key is to remain adaptable while keeping your long-term vision intact.

1. Being Open to Change

Your financial plan is not set in stone. As your income, expenses, or financial priorities shift, your plan may need to be revised to reflect your current situation. Whether you're facing a change in employment, a new financial responsibility, or an economic downturn, being open to adjusting your plan allows you to stay on track despite the changes.

Proverbs 16:9 says, "In their hearts humans plan their course, but the Lord establishes their steps." This verse reminds us that while we can plan, we must also be flexible enough to adapt as new circumstances arise. Financial plans are meant to be dynamic, evolving as you grow and as life changes.

For example, if your income decreases unexpectedly, you may need to reduce your savings or delay certain financial goals temporarily. Adjusting your plan doesn't mean giving up—it means recalibrating to ensure that you stay on course toward your long-term objectives.

2. Revisiting and Refining Your Goals

Periodically reviewing your financial goals is an essential part of staying consistent. Over time, your goals may change, and it's important to refine them to reflect your current values and priorities. Philippians 3:13-14 reminds us to keep pressing forward: "Forgetting what is behind and straining toward what is ahead, I press on toward the goal to win the prize for which God has called me heavenward in Christ Jesus."

Revisiting your goals helps you to stay focused on what truly matters, while also allowing you to refine your approach as needed. This can include adjusting timelines, setting new financial targets, or prioritizing different aspects of your financial plan based on changing circumstances.

3. Keeping Your Long-Term Vision Intact

While flexibility is important, it's equally essential to keep your long-term vision intact. Your goals may need to be adjusted along the way, but your commitment to financial success should remain unwavering. Habakkuk 2:3 encourages patience in the pursuit of our vision: "For the vision is yet for an appointed time; but at the end it shall speak, and not lie: though it tarry, wait for it; because it will surely come, it will not tarry."

Staying focused on the big picture helps you to maintain perspective during temporary setbacks or adjustments. Even when you need to alter your plan, keeping your end goal in mind ensures that you continue making progress toward financial success. Consistency doesn't mean never changing your approach—it means staying true to your vision no matter what.

The Power of Consistency and Adaptability

Consistency is the driving force behind financial success. It is the daily, weekly, and monthly commitment to your financial plan that leads to long-term results. By developing financial habits, staying focused through challenges, and celebrating small victories along the way, you build momentum toward your financial goals.

At the same time, flexibility is essential. Life changes, and your financial plan must change with it. Adjusting your plan as needed allows you to navigate unexpected circumstances without losing sight of your long-term vision. Proverbs 3:5-6 reminds us, "Trust in the Lord with all your heart and lean not on your own understanding; in all your

ways submit to Him, and He will make your paths straight."
By trusting God's guidance and remaining consistent in your
actions, you can achieve financial success while adapting to
life's changes.

Stay committed, stay adaptable, and keep your eyes on
the prize. Your consistent efforts, guided by faith and
wisdom, will lead you to the financial success you seek.

CHAPTER 07

OVERCOMING OBSTRACLES

Dealing with Financial Setbacks

In any journey toward financial success, obstacles and setbacks are inevitable. Whether it's an unexpected expense, a failed investment, or a sudden economic downturn, setbacks can challenge even the most well-thought-out financial plans. However, setbacks don't have to be the end of the story. In fact, they can be the catalyst for growth and learning, providing invaluable lessons that propel you forward on the path to wealth. This chapter will explore how to turn financial failures into learning opportunities and emphasize the critical role that perseverance plays in achieving long-term wealth.

How to Turn Failures into Learning Opportunities

Every successful person encounters failures along the way, but the key difference between those who achieve lasting financial success and those who do not is how they respond to these failures. Instead of viewing setbacks as final, successful people use failures as learning opportunities and stepping stones toward greater success.

1. Acknowledge and Analyze the Setback

The first step in turning a failure into a learning opportunity is to acknowledge it. Denying or ignoring financial setbacks only prolongs the pain and prevents you from learning the important lessons they offer. Once you've acknowledged the setback, take time to analyze what went wrong. Did you overspend in certain areas? Was an investment decision made without enough research? Did unexpected circumstances arise that you hadn't planned for?

Proverbs 12:1 says, "Whoever loves discipline loves knowledge, but whoever hates correction is stupid." This verse reminds us that accepting correction and learning from mistakes is a sign of wisdom. Rather than beating yourself up over what went wrong, view the setback as a necessary part of the journey and use it as an opportunity to gain insight into how you can improve moving forward.

2. Extract the Lessons

Every failure carries valuable lessons that can inform future decisions. Ask yourself, "What can I learn from this situation that will help me make better choices in the future?"

Perhaps a failed investment teaches you the importance of diversification, or an overspending problem highlights the need for stricter budgeting. Once you've identified the lessons, take note of them and apply them to your future financial strategies.

Proverbs 24:16 encourages resilience by stating, "For though the righteous fall seven times, they rise again, but the wicked stumble when calamity strikes." This verse highlights that even those who are wise and faithful may fall, but they get back up each time. Use each setback as an opportunity to rise stronger and wiser than before.

3. Develop a Growth Mindset

A growth mindset is the belief that abilities and intelligence can be developed through effort, learning, and perseverance. When you approach financial setbacks with a growth mindset, you see challenges as opportunities to grow and improve, rather than as permanent failures. People with a growth mindset are more likely to bounce back from financial difficulties because they view every obstacle as a learning experience.

James 1:2-3 says, "Consider it pure joy, my brothers and sisters, whenever you face trials of many kinds, because you know that the testing of your faith produces perseverance." Adopting a growth mindset helps you to embrace setbacks with a positive attitude, knowing that each challenge is shaping you into a stronger, more capable person.

4. Adjust Your Strategy

Once you've extracted the lessons from your setback, adjust your financial strategy accordingly. This may involve refining your budget, rethinking your investment approach, or reassessing your financial goals. The key is to take actionable steps based on what you've learned. Failure is only valuable if it leads to positive change. By adjusting your strategy, you ensure that your setbacks propel you forward rather than hold you back.

Proverbs 16:3 reminds us to commit our plans to God: "Commit to the Lord whatever you do, and He will establish your plans." By adjusting your plans based on what you've learned and seeking God's guidance, you create a more resilient financial strategy that aligns with His wisdom.

The Role of Perseverance in Achieving Wealth

Perseverance is one of the most important qualities for achieving financial success. It is the ability to keep moving forward, even when the path becomes difficult, and the resolve to stay committed to your financial goals, regardless of the obstacles in your way. Perseverance turns temporary setbacks into opportunities for growth and ensures that you stay on course toward long-term wealth.

1. The Power of Persistence

Achieving wealth is not an overnight process; it requires long-term commitment and consistent effort. There will be moments when progress seems slow or when challenges make you question whether your efforts are worth it. However, it is in these moments that perseverance becomes crucial.

Galatians 6:9 offers encouragement for persistence: "Let us not become weary in doing good, for at the proper time we will reap a harvest if we do not give up." This verse reminds us that while the rewards of our efforts may not be immediate, they will come in due time if we remain faithful to the process. Persistence in saving, investing, and managing money wisely will eventually lead to financial success, even if the journey is difficult.

2. Building Resilience Through Challenges

Perseverance builds resilience, which is the ability to bounce back from adversity and continue moving forward. Financial setbacks, such as job loss, market crashes, or unexpected expenses, can be discouraging, but they also offer the opportunity to develop resilience. Each time you overcome a financial challenge, you strengthen your ability to handle future obstacles with confidence.

Romans 5:3-4 emphasizes the value of perseverance: "Not only so, but we also glory in our sufferings, because we know that suffering produces perseverance; perseverance, character; and character, hope." As you persevere through financial difficulties, your character is shaped, and you gain the hope and confidence to continue striving for your goals.

3. Focusing on Long-Term Success

Perseverance requires a long-term perspective. When setbacks occur, it's easy to become discouraged and lose sight of your goals, but focusing on the bigger picture helps you stay committed. Wealth creation is a marathon, not a sprint, and those who stay the course are the ones who ultimately succeed.

Hebrews 12:1 encourages us to run the race with endurance: "Let us run with perseverance the race marked out for us, fixing our eyes on Jesus, the pioneer and perfecter of faith." In the same way, financial success requires perseverance as you keep your eyes on the long-term vision. Short-term setbacks are part of the process, but they do not define the outcome if you stay committed to your goals.

4. Celebrating Small Victories

Celebrating small victories along the way can help maintain motivation and perseverance. Whether it's reaching a savings milestone, paying off a portion of debt, or successfully navigating a financial challenge, recognizing and celebrating progress fuels your determination to keep going.

Nehemiah 8:10 reminds us that "The joy of the Lord is your strength." Finding joy in your journey and celebrating small wins can provide the emotional and spiritual strength needed to persevere through difficult times. Each step forward, no matter how small, brings you closer to your ultimate goal.

Perseverance Through Setbacks Leads to Success

Financial setbacks are inevitable, but they do not have to define your journey. By viewing failures as learning opportunities and embracing a mindset of perseverance, you can turn every challenge into a stepping stone toward success. The road to wealth is not always smooth, but with persistence, resilience, and a long-term perspective, you can overcome obstacles and achieve financial prosperity.

As you face challenges along your financial journey, remember the words of Philippians 4:13: "I can do all this through him who gives me strength." With faith, perseverance, and a willingness to learn from setbacks, you can navigate any obstacle and continue moving toward your financial goals.

Mindset Shifts for Overcoming Financial Challenges

Changing Your Perspective on Money Problems

Financial challenges are a common part of life, and how you approach them determines whether they hold you back or propel you forward. One of the most effective ways to overcome financial challenges is by shifting your mindset. Instead of viewing money problems as obstacles, you can begin to see them as opportunities for growth, learning, and improvement. By transforming your thinking, you unlock the potential to not only overcome financial setbacks but to thrive in the face of them.

1. See Problems as Opportunities for Growth

The first step in shifting your mindset is to stop seeing money problems as permanent roadblocks and start viewing them as opportunities to grow. Every financial challenge, whether it's managing debt, facing unexpected expenses, or navigating economic downturns, contains a lesson that can strengthen your financial acumen. Challenges teach you to be resourceful, creative, and disciplined—traits that are essential for long-term wealth.

Romans 8:28 says, "And we know that in all things God works for the good of those who love him, who have been called according to his purpose." This verse reminds us that even in difficult situations, God is working for our good. Financial problems can be a tool that refines your character and builds the strength needed for future success. By shifting your perspective to see challenges as stepping stones rather than stumbling blocks, you transform how you approach financial issues.

2. Focus on What You Can Control

Financial challenges often come with a sense of helplessness or frustration, especially when circumstances feel beyond your control. However, shifting your mindset involves focusing on what you can control, rather than what you cannot. While you may not be able to control external factors like market downturns, job losses, or rising costs of living, you do have control over how you respond to these situations.

Philippians 4:6-7 advises us, "Do not be anxious about anything, but in every situation, by prayer and petition, with thanksgiving, present your requests to God. And the peace of God, which transcends all understanding, will guard your hearts and your minds in Christ Jesus." Focusing on what you can control reduces anxiety and helps you direct your energy toward productive solutions. This includes managing your budget, reducing unnecessary expenses, exploring new income streams, and improving your financial literacy.

3. Cultivate a Positive, Abundance-Based Mindset

A scarcity mindset focuses on lack and limitation, while an abundance mindset emphasizes opportunity, growth, and potential. Shifting from a scarcity mindset to an abundance mindset is crucial for overcoming financial challenges. When you operate from a mindset of scarcity, you may feel fearful, hold back from taking risks, or miss opportunities for growth. However, an abundance mindset sees possibilities even in difficult circumstances and opens the door to creative solutions.

Proverbs 11:24-25 teaches, "One person gives freely, yet gains even more; another withholds unduly, but comes to poverty. A generous person will prosper; whoever refreshes others will be refreshed." This passage illustrates the paradox of abundance: when you focus on giving, sharing, and expanding, you attract more into your life. Adopting an abundance mindset encourages you to approach financial challenges with creativity and optimism, rather than fear.

Developing Resilience and Adaptability

Resilience and adaptability are essential qualities for navigating financial challenges. Resilience is the ability to bounce back from adversity, while adaptability is the capacity to adjust to new circumstances and thrive in changing environments. By developing these qualities, you empower yourself to overcome setbacks and continue progressing toward your financial goals.

1. Build Emotional Resilience

Emotional resilience is the ability to stay calm, focused, and positive in the face of financial difficulties. It helps you manage stress and maintain perspective when things don't go as planned. One of the ways to build emotional resilience is through practicing gratitude and maintaining a hopeful outlook. Gratitude shifts your focus from what you lack to what you already have, which strengthens your emotional resilience.

James 1:2-4 encourages us to embrace trials with joy: "Consider it pure joy, my brothers and sisters, whenever you face trials of many kinds, because you know that the testing of your faith produces perseverance. Let perseverance finish its work so that you may be mature and complete, not lacking anything." By seeing challenges as opportunities to grow in perseverance and maturity, you develop the emotional strength needed to navigate financial hardships.

Practical ways to build emotional resilience include:

- Keeping a gratitude journal to focus on the positives in your life.

- Seeking support from friends, family, or mentors who can offer encouragement.

- Engaging in activities like prayer, meditation, or exercise to reduce stress.

2. Develop Financial Adaptability

Financial adaptability is the ability to adjust your financial strategy when circumstances change. This may involve revising your budget, exploring new sources of income, or shifting your investment strategy. Adaptability ensures that when faced with a setback, you can quickly pivot and find new solutions rather than becoming stuck.

Proverbs 24:10 reminds us, "If you falter in a time of trouble, how small is your strength!" This verse emphasizes the importance of staying strong and flexible in difficult times. Financial challenges may require you to adapt by cutting non-essential expenses, downsizing, or exploring new financial opportunities, such as freelancing or starting a side business. Being adaptable allows you to weather financial storms while staying focused on your long-term goals.

3. Strengthen Problem-Solving Skills

Another key aspect of overcoming financial challenges is strengthening your problem-solving skills. Financial obstacles often require creative thinking and innovation. Instead of seeing financial problems as insurmountable, view them as puzzles to solve. This shift in mindset encourages you to explore different options, seek advice, and think outside the box.

Proverbs 2:6-7 says, "For the LORD gives wisdom; from his mouth come knowledge and understanding. He holds success in store for the upright, he is a shield to those whose walk is blameless." By seeking wisdom and understanding, you can develop the problem-solving skills necessary to overcome financial challenges. Whether it's negotiating better terms with creditors, finding new investment opportunities, or developing a new budget strategy, a problem-solving approach helps you find solutions in difficult situations.

4. Learn to Embrace Change

Financial challenges often come with significant change, whether it's a shift in your income, career, or financial responsibilities. Embracing change with a positive mindset and a willingness to adapt is crucial for long-term success. Change can be uncomfortable, but it often opens doors to new opportunities.

Ecclesiastes 3:1 reminds us that there is a time for everything: "There is a time for everything, and a season for every activity under the heavens." Just as life has seasons, your financial journey will have seasons of growth, challenge, and transformation. Embracing these seasons and being willing to adapt allows you to move through financial challenges with grace and resilience.

The Power of Mindset in Overcoming Financial Challenges

Overcoming financial challenges requires more than just practical solutions; it requires a shift in mindset. By changing how you view money problems and developing resilience and adaptability, you can turn financial setbacks into opportunities for growth and success. Romans 12:2 reminds us, "Do not conform to the pattern of this world, but be transformed by the renewing of your mind." When you renew your mind and approach financial challenges with a positive, growth-oriented perspective, you unlock new possibilities and build the resilience needed for long-term wealth.

As you continue your financial journey, remember that challenges are not permanent roadblocks but opportunities to learn, grow, and adapt. By cultivating a mindset of abundance, focusing on what you can control, and developing resilience, you can overcome any financial obstacle and move closer to achieving your financial goals.

CHAPTER 08

THE ROLE OF ACTION

Taking Action on Your Ideas

Ideas are the seeds of wealth, but they can only take root and grow when paired with action. No matter how brilliant or creative your ideas are, without action, they remain nothing more than untapped potential. The key to wealth creation lies in your ability to take consistent and deliberate action toward your financial goals. This chapter will explore the importance of execution in wealth creation and how you can move from thought to action.

The Importance of Execution in Wealth Creation

Many people have great ideas, whether it's a business venture, an investment opportunity, or a creative solution to a financial problem. However, the difference between those who succeed and those who don't lies in the ability to turn those ideas into action. Execution is what transforms thoughts and plans into results, and without it, even the best ideas will fail to bring financial success.

1. Ideas Alone Do Not Build Wealth

Ideas are valuable, but they must be paired with execution to generate wealth. For example, you may have a brilliant idea for a new product or service, but until you take the necessary steps to develop, market, and sell that product, it will never bring you financial success. Similarly, an idea for a new investment strategy is useless if you don't act on it by making investments.

James 2:17 says, "Faith by itself, if it is not accompanied by action, is dead." This principle applies to wealth creation as well. Faith in your ideas and financial goals is crucial, but it must be backed by action. Without taking steps to bring your ideas to life, they will remain dormant, and opportunities will be lost.

2. Action Creates Momentum

Taking action, even in small steps, creates momentum. Once you begin moving toward your financial goals, you build the energy and motivation needed to continue progressing. Action also opens the door to opportunities that might not have been visible when your ideas were still just concepts.

Proverbs 14:23 reminds us of the value of effort: "All hard work brings a profit, but mere talk leads only to poverty." This verse highlights that work and action are essential for bringing profit. No matter how small the steps may seem, each action brings you closer to your goal and creates the momentum needed for long-term success.

3. Overcoming the Fear of Failure

One of the main reasons people hesitate to take action on their ideas is the fear of failure. They worry that their efforts might not lead to success or that they will make mistakes along the way. However, fear of failure is one of the greatest barriers to wealth creation. Action involves risk, but without it, there can be no reward.

Ecclesiastes 11:4 says, "Whoever watches the wind will not plant; whoever looks at the clouds will not reap." This verse teaches us that waiting for perfect conditions will result in missed opportunities. If you wait until you feel completely ready or until all risks are eliminated, you will never take the action needed to create wealth. Instead, recognize that failure is a natural part of the process, and each setback provides a learning opportunity that moves you closer to success.

Moving from Thought to Action

Moving from thought to action requires more than just desire; it involves planning, discipline, and a willingness to take risks. Here are key steps to help you move from idea to execution:

1. Break Down Big Ideas into Actionable Steps

Big financial goals or ideas can feel overwhelming, but by breaking them down into smaller, actionable steps, you make them more manageable. Instead of focusing on the entire goal at once, focus on what you can do today, this week, or this month to move closer to your objective.

For example, if your idea is to start a new business, break the process down into steps such as writing a business plan, conducting market research, setting up a website, and marketing your products. Each step is a piece of the larger puzzle, and by focusing on one task at a time, you make progress without feeling overwhelmed.

Proverbs 16:9 reminds us, "In their hearts humans plan their course, but the Lord establishes their steps." Planning and taking small steps allow God to guide and establish your progress toward success.

2. Create a Daily or Weekly Action Plan

Consistency is key when moving from thought to action. Create a daily or weekly action plan that outlines the specific tasks you need to complete to bring your ideas to life. This plan acts as a guide, keeping you on track and helping you prioritize the actions that matter most.

Each day, focus on completing at least one task that moves you closer to your financial goals. Whether it's making an investment, building your savings, or learning a new skill, consistent action builds momentum. Luke 16:10 says, "Whoever can be trusted with very little can also be trusted with much." The small, daily actions you take build a foundation for greater opportunities and success.

3. Seek Accountability and Support

Taking action can be challenging, especially when you're facing uncertainty or stepping into new territory. To stay motivated, seek accountability and support from others. Whether it's a mentor, a friend, or a financial advisor, having someone to check in with can help you stay focused and committed to your goals.

Ecclesiastes 4:9-10 teaches the value of partnership: "Two are better than one, because they have a good return for their labor: If either of them falls down, one can help the other up." Surrounding yourself with supportive individuals ensures that you have guidance and encouragement when challenges arise, helping you continue moving forward.

4. Measure and Celebrate Progress

As you take action toward your financial goals, it's important to measure your progress regularly. This allows you to see how far you've come and identify any areas where adjustments may be needed. Celebrate small wins along the way, as this reinforces the positive effects of your actions and keeps you motivated.

Proverbs 27:23 advises us, "Be sure you know the condition of your flocks, give careful attention to your herds." In the same way, pay close attention to your financial progress. Review your results, track your actions, and celebrate each milestone you achieve. These celebrations remind you that your efforts are producing results and encourage you to keep moving forward.

5. Adapt and Learn from Experience

Taking action doesn't guarantee immediate success, and you may encounter setbacks along the way. However, each step you take provides valuable experience and insight. Be willing to adapt your approach when necessary, and don't be discouraged by challenges. Instead, use them as learning opportunities to refine your strategy and continue progressing.

Proverbs 24:16 reminds us that, "For though the righteous fall seven times, they rise again." This verse emphasizes resilience in the face of setbacks. Keep taking action, even if you stumble along the way. Each time you rise, you grow stronger, wiser, and more prepared to succeed.

The Power of Action in Wealth Creation

Wealth creation requires more than just ideas and plans—it requires action. Execution is the bridge between thought and success, and without it, even the best ideas will remain unfulfilled. By taking deliberate, consistent action, breaking down large goals into manageable steps, and embracing the process of learning and adapting, you can turn your ideas into reality.

As you move forward on your financial journey, remember the words of James 2:26: "As the body without the spirit is dead, so faith without deeds is dead." Faith in your ideas and goals is important, but it must be paired with action to produce results. By moving from thought to action, you set yourself on the path to achieving the wealth and success you desire.

The Power of Small Steps

How Small, Consistent Actions Lead to Big Financial Gains

When we think about wealth creation, it's easy to get caught up in the idea of big, dramatic moves—whether it's launching a lucrative business or landing a significant investment opportunity. While large financial decisions can play a role in success, the true power lies in small, consistent actions. These small steps, when taken regularly, compound over time and lead to significant financial gains. It's not the size of each action that matters, but the consistency with which those actions are taken.

1. The Power of Compounding

One of the most remarkable principles of financial growth is compounding. This concept applies not only to investments but also to the small actions we take every day. Whether it's saving a portion of your income, paying down debt, or consistently investing, each small step builds upon the last. Over time, the cumulative effect of these actions leads to substantial financial growth.

Proverbs 13:11 says, "Dishonest money dwindles away, but whoever gathers money little by little makes it grow." This verse highlights the importance of steady, consistent efforts in building wealth. The key to compounding is time and patience—small, regular contributions grow exponentially over time. Even modest savings, when invested wisely, can lead to significant financial rewards.

2. Building Financial Momentum

Small, consistent actions also create momentum. When you begin making positive financial decisions, each action reinforces the next. For example, when you start saving regularly, you not only build your savings account, but you also build confidence in your ability to manage your finances effectively. This confidence motivates you to continue taking positive steps, such as investing or paying off debt.

Zechariah 4:10 encourages us not to despise small beginnings: "Who dares despise the day of small things?" Even the smallest financial steps can set you on a path to greater success. Over time, these small actions snowball, leading to significant progress and momentum that drives you toward your financial goals.

3. Consistency Over Intensity

The key to financial success isn't found in one-time, intense efforts but in consistent actions over time. While occasional large financial moves can be helpful, it is the daily discipline of managing money that ultimately creates long-term wealth. Whether it's contributing to your retirement account, sticking to a budget, or consistently paying off debt, regular, focused effort produces results.

Proverbs 21:5 reminds us, "The plans of the diligent lead to profit as surely as haste leads to poverty." Diligence—steady, persistent effort—leads to profit. Financial habits, no matter how small, build a foundation of wealth over time.

Developing Daily Habits That Promote Wealth

To harness the power of small steps, it's important to develop daily habits that support your financial goals. These habits don't need to be complicated or time-consuming;

rather, they should be simple, repeatable actions that you can integrate into your routine. Over time, these habits will become second nature, consistently pushing you closer to your financial objectives.

1. Track Your Spending Daily

One of the most fundamental habits for building wealth is tracking your spending. By monitoring where your money goes each day, you gain control over your finances and can make informed decisions. Small, daily expenses can quickly add up, and without regular tracking, you may find yourself spending more than you realize.

By creating the habit of reviewing your expenses every day, you become more mindful of your spending patterns and are better equipped to make adjustments when necessary. Proverbs 27:23 teaches us the value of paying attention to our resources: "Be sure you know the condition of your flocks, give careful attention to your herds." In modern terms, this means staying on top of your finances to ensure that you're making wise decisions.

2. Save a Portion of Every Paycheck

One of the simplest and most effective ways to build wealth is by saving a portion of every paycheck. Even if it's a small percentage, saving consistently over time allows your money to grow. Whether you set aside 5%, 10%, or more, the habit of regular saving is key to long-term financial success.

Proverbs 6:6-8 offers wisdom from the ant's example: "Go to the ant, you sluggard; consider its ways and be wise! It has no commander, no overseer or ruler, yet it stores its provisions in summer and gathers its food at harvest." Like the ant, develop the habit of saving consistently, so that you are prepared for the future and can capitalize on opportunities that come your way.

3. Pay Down Debt Incrementally

Debt can be one of the biggest obstacles to wealth creation, but by developing the habit of paying it down incrementally, you can steadily reduce your liabilities. Even small extra payments toward debt can make a significant impact over time by reducing the interest you pay and accelerating your path to financial freedom.

Create a habit of making small, additional payments each month—whether it's paying a little extra on your credit card balance or adding to your student loan payments. Over time, these small steps will reduce your debt load and free up more money for saving and investing.

4. Invest Regularly, No Matter the Amount

Many people hesitate to invest because they feel they don't have enough money to make a meaningful difference. However, investing small amounts consistently can lead to significant growth over time. Whether through a retirement account, stocks, or other investment vehicles, making regular contributions—even if they are small—allows you to benefit from the power of compounding.

Ecclesiastes 11:2 encourages diversification in investments: "Invest in seven ventures, yes, in eight; you do not know what disaster may come upon the land." By developing the habit of investing regularly, you build

wealth slowly but steadily. Over time, your small contributions, combined with compound interest, can result in substantial financial growth. The key is consistency—invest regularly, no matter the amount, and allow your investments to grow over the long term.

5. Review Your Financial Goals Regularly

Another powerful habit for promoting wealth is reviewing your financial goals on a regular basis. This ensures that you stay focused and aligned with your long-term objectives. Whether it's checking in on your progress monthly or quarterly, reviewing your goals helps you remain accountable and allows you to adjust your strategy if necessary.

Proverbs 16:3 advises, "Commit to the LORD whatever you do, and He will establish your plans." By committing your financial goals to God and regularly reviewing them, you reinforce your dedication to achieving them. This practice keeps your goals top of mind and motivates you to take small, consistent steps toward their achievement.

6. Practice Gratitude for Financial Progress

Cultivating an attitude of gratitude for even the smallest financial wins can help you stay motivated and focused. Instead of becoming discouraged by how far you still have to go, recognize and celebrate the progress you've made. This positive mindset can fuel your determination and make the journey to financial success more enjoyable.

1 Thessalonians 5:18 encourages gratitude: "Give thanks in all circumstances; for this is God's will for you in Christ Jesus." By focusing on what you have achieved rather than what you lack, you maintain a positive outlook and attract further abundance into your life.

Small Steps Lead to Big Financial Gains

The journey to wealth is not about sudden leaps but about the power of small, consistent actions taken over time. By developing daily habits that support your financial goals—such as saving, investing, paying down debt, and reviewing your progress—you lay the foundation for long-term financial success. These habits may seem small, but their cumulative effect leads to significant gains, much like how water steadily erodes rock over time.

Remember the wisdom of Proverbs 13:11: "Wealth gained hastily will dwindle, but whoever gathers money little by little makes it grow." Each small, deliberate step you take moves you closer to financial freedom and stability.

As you continue your financial journey, embrace the power of small steps. Commit to daily habits that promote wealth, trust in the process, and watch as your small actions compound into big financial rewards.

CHAPTER 09

THE SEED OF WEALTH

Planting the Idea of Wealth

Wealth is often seen as something that exists in the physical world—money in the bank, investments, properties, or material possessions. However, true wealth begins long before it is physically realized; it starts as a seed planted in the mind. This seed, the idea of wealth, grows through careful nurturing, belief, and action. Cultivating a wealthy mindset is the foundation for long-term financial success. In this chapter, we will explore how to plant the seed of wealth in your mind and how to nurture it into a prosperous reality.

How to Cultivate a Wealthy Mindset

A wealthy mindset is not defined solely by the amount of money you have, but by the way you think about money, opportunities, and abundance. The mindset you carry influences your financial decisions, your habits, and your approach to challenges. By cultivating a mindset of abundance, growth, and possibility, you lay the groundwork for lasting wealth.

1. Shift from Scarcity to Abundance

The first step in cultivating a wealthy mindset is shifting your thinking from a scarcity mentality to an abundance mentality. A scarcity mindset is rooted in fear, limitation, and the belief that resources are finite. This type of thinking leads to behaviors like hoarding money, avoiding risk, and focusing on what you don't have. In contrast, an abundance mindset is focused on growth, opportunity, and the belief that there is more than enough to go around.

Philippians 4:19 says, "And my God will meet all your needs according to the riches of his glory in Christ Jesus." This verse reminds us that God's provision is limitless and that there is no need to operate out of fear or scarcity. Embracing an abundance mindset allows you to see opportunities where others see lack and opens the door to greater financial success.

2. Focus on Growth, Not Just Accumulation

A wealthy mindset is not just about accumulating money but about growth in every area of life—spiritually, mentally, and financially. Instead of fixating on amassing wealth for wealth's sake, focus on growing your knowledge, skills, and understanding of wealth creation. As you grow, your capacity to generate and manage wealth expands as well.

Proverbs 4:7 reminds us of the importance of wisdom: "The beginning of wisdom is this: Get wisdom. Though it cost all you have, get understanding." Gaining wisdom and understanding in financial matters allows you to make smarter decisions that lead to long-term wealth. Cultivate a mindset that prioritizes continuous learning and growth over merely accumulating wealth.

3. Visualize Success

Visualization is a powerful tool in cultivating a wealthy mindset. By picturing yourself achieving financial success, you condition your mind to believe that it is possible. Visualization helps you clarify your goals, stay focused, and act as though success is already within reach. This mental rehearsal trains your subconscious mind to align your thoughts, behaviors, and decisions with your vision of wealth.

Proverbs 23:7 says, "For as he thinks in his heart, so is he." This verse underscores the power of thought in shaping your reality. By consistently visualizing financial success and acting in accordance with that vision, you begin to manifest the wealth you desire. Visualizing your success helps you overcome doubts and stay motivated, even when obstacles arise.

4. Practice Gratitude for What You Have

Gratitude is an essential part of a wealthy mindset. By focusing on what you already have, rather than what you lack, you cultivate contentment and attract more abundance into your life. Gratitude shifts your mindset from scarcity to abundance and reminds you of the blessings and resources already available to you.

1 Thessalonians 5:18 advises, "Give thanks in all circumstances; for this is God's will for you in Christ Jesus." When you practice gratitude, you open your heart and mind to receive even more. Cultivating an attitude of gratitude for your current financial situation, no matter how small or modest, sets the stage for greater wealth to come.

5. Believe in Your Ability to Create Wealth

Cultivating a wealthy mindset also requires faith in your own abilities. Believe that you have the potential to create wealth, even if you haven't yet seen the results. Your belief in your financial potential is what motivates you to take action, persevere through challenges, and seize opportunities.

Deuteronomy 8:18 says, "But remember the LORD your God, for it is he who gives you the ability to produce wealth." Recognizing that your ability to create wealth comes from God strengthens your belief that financial success is possible. When you believe in your potential, you are more likely to take bold actions that lead to wealth creation.

Understanding That Wealth Begins in the Mind

Wealth is more than just a collection of material possessions; it is a state of mind. The way you think about money, opportunities, and success has a direct impact on the wealth you create. Your thoughts influence your decisions, behaviors, and the opportunities you see around you. If you believe that wealth is possible for you and that you have the power to create it, you will take actions that align with that belief. If you believe that wealth is out of your reach, your actions (or lack of action) will reflect that belief as well.

1. Mindset Shapes Financial Behavior

Your mindset dictates how you approach financial decisions. Those with a wealthy mindset tend to approach money with confidence, viewing it as a tool to be used wisely and effectively. They are willing to take calculated risks, invest in opportunities, and think long term. In contrast, those with a scarcity mindset may avoid risk, focus on short-term gains, or become paralyzed by fear of losing money.

Romans 12:2 encourages a transformed mind: "Do not conform to the pattern of this world, but be transformed by the renewing of your mind." Renewing your mind to think about wealth from a position of faith, abundance, and wisdom transforms how you approach financial decisions. Instead of being driven by fear or anxiety, you can make decisions based on growth, opportunity, and long-term success.

2. Belief Creates Reality

The idea that wealth begins in the mind is supported by both spiritual and psychological principles. What you believe about yourself and your financial potential will eventually manifest in your reality. If you believe that financial success is beyond your reach, your actions will reflect that belief, leading to missed opportunities and limited growth. However, if you believe that wealth is possible for you, your actions will align with that belief, opening the door to financial success.

Mark 9:23 reminds us, "Everything is possible for one who believes." When you believe in the possibility of wealth and align your mindset with that belief, you create the conditions for success. Your belief shapes your reality, and by planting the seed of wealth in your mind, you take the first step toward realizing your financial goals.

3. Nurturing the Seed of Wealth

Just as a seed needs water, sunlight, and care to grow, the seed of wealth in your mind needs to be nurtured through positive thoughts, consistent action, and faith. Cultivating a wealthy mindset is an ongoing process that requires daily attention and effort. By feeding your mind with wisdom, staying focused on your goals, and taking small steps each day, you nurture the seed of wealth and allow it to grow into a flourishing financial future.

Proverbs 24:27 advises, "Put your outdoor work in order and get your fields ready; after that, build your house." This verse teaches us the importance of preparation and nurturing the resources we have. In the same way, nurturing the seed of wealth in your mind ensures that your financial future is well-prepared and ready to thrive.

Planting the Seed of Wealth

Wealth begins as an idea, a seed planted in your mind. By cultivating a wealthy mindset—one rooted in abundance, growth, and faith—you create the foundation for long-term financial success. The thoughts you nurture and the beliefs you hold about wealth shape your actions, which in turn shape your financial reality.

Remember the wisdom of Proverbs 23:7: "For as he thinks in his heart, so is he." By planting the idea of wealth in your mind and nurturing it through consistent effort, visualization, and belief, you set yourself on the path to realizing your financial goals. Wealth is not just something you acquire—it's something you create, starting with the mindset you cultivate today.

Harvesting Abundance

The Process of Reaping the Rewards of Your Financial Ideas

Just as a farmer plants seeds with the expectation of a future harvest, your financial journey begins with planting the seeds of wealth through ideas, actions, and habits. After seasons of nurturing, disciplined effort, and consistent work, the time comes to reap the rewards of your financial ideas. This is the moment when your diligent planning, sacrifices, and persistence yield tangible results, allowing you to experience financial abundance.

1. Recognizing the Season of Harvest

The harvest is the result of a long period of preparation, growth, and cultivation. In financial terms, it's the moment when your investments mature, your savings reach significant milestones, or your business becomes profitable. However, just as in farming, the timing of the harvest is crucial. Recognizing when it's time to reap the rewards of your efforts requires wisdom and patience.

Ecclesiastes 3:1 reminds us, "There is a time for everything, and a season for every activity under the heavens." Just as there is a season for planting, there is a season for harvesting. In your financial life, this means understanding when it's time to withdraw from your investments, enjoy the fruits of your labor, or take calculated risks that bring your financial goals to fruition. The season of harvest comes after consistent work, and it requires discernment to know when to reap the rewards.

2. Enjoying the Fruits of Your Labor

Harvesting abundance isn't just about financial gains; it's also about enjoying the process and celebrating the success you've worked so hard to achieve. After years of diligent saving, investing, or building a business, taking the time to appreciate and enjoy your financial success is important. Whether it's taking a long-planned vacation, buying a home, or simply enjoying the peace of financial stability, celebrating your achievements is a vital part of harvesting abundance.

Psalm 128:2 says, "You will eat the fruit of your labor; blessings and prosperity will be yours." This verse emphasizes that enjoying the rewards of your hard work is a blessing. It's important to allow yourself to enjoy the fruits of your labor without guilt or hesitation, knowing that you have earned your success through disciplined efforts and wise financial decisions.

3. Reaping Financial Growth from Investments

One of the most powerful aspects of financial abundance is the growth that comes from your investments. Whether you've invested in stocks, real estate, or a business, the time comes when your money begins to work for you, producing returns without the need for additional effort. This is the true power of financial independence—when your investments generate enough income to sustain your lifestyle and allow you to focus on new opportunities.

Proverbs 3:9-10 encourages us to honor God with our wealth: "Honor the LORD with your wealth, with the firstfruits of all your crops; then your barns will be filled to overflowing, and your vats will brim over with new wine." When you experience financial growth from your investments, it's a time to recognize the blessings that come from wise stewardship and to use your resources for good.

Celebrating Financial Success and Reinvesting for Future Wealth

Celebrating your financial success is important, but it's equally critical to continue planting seeds for future wealth. The process of building financial abundance is ongoing— harvesting today's success doesn't mean the work is done. It's essential to reinvest part of your harvest to ensure that your financial future remains secure and that you continue to grow your wealth.

1. Celebrate Your Wins with Gratitude

Achieving financial success is no small feat, and it's important to take time to celebrate the milestones along your journey. Whether it's paying off a major debt, reaching a significant savings goal, or seeing your business thrive, celebrating your wins with gratitude helps reinforce the positive behaviors and decisions that led to your success.

Deuteronomy 8:18 reminds us, "But remember the LORD your God, for it is He who gives you the ability to produce wealth." As you celebrate your financial success, remember to give thanks for the opportunities, guidance, and resources that made it possible. Gratitude helps you stay grounded and focused on using your wealth wisely and responsibly.

2. Reinvest for Continued Growth

While it's important to enjoy the rewards of your financial success, it's equally crucial to reinvest part of your wealth to ensure continued growth. Reinvesting your money—whether it's in the stock market, real estate, or a business—allows you to multiply your resources and secure financial stability for the future.

Proverbs 13:22 says, "A good person leaves an inheritance for their children's children, but a sinner's wealth is stored up for the righteous." Reinvesting your wealth not only ensures your own financial security but also creates opportunities for future generations. By continuing to plant seeds even after a successful harvest, you set the stage for ongoing financial abundance that benefits both you and your family.

3. Diversify and Expand Your Financial Portfolio

Harvesting abundance also presents an opportunity to diversify and expand your financial portfolio. Instead of relying solely on one income stream or investment, consider exploring new opportunities that align with your financial goals. Whether it's investing in different industries, starting a new business venture, or exploring passive income opportunities, diversifying your investments allows you to spread risk and increase your potential for long-term success.

Ecclesiastes 11:6 offers wisdom on diversification: "Sow your seed in the morning, and at evening let your hands not be idle, for you do not know which will succeed, whether this or that, or whether both will do equally well." By reinvesting and diversifying your portfolio, you create multiple avenues for wealth creation, ensuring that you continue to reap rewards in the future.

4. Share Your Abundance with Others

One of the most rewarding aspects of financial success is the ability to give back and help others. Sharing your abundance through charitable giving, supporting causes you care about, or helping those in need not only blesses others but also brings fulfillment and purpose to your financial journey.

2 Corinthians 9:6 encourages generosity: "Remember this: Whoever sows sparingly will also reap sparingly, and whoever sows generously will also reap generously." By sharing your wealth generously, you contribute to the well-being of others and align your financial success with a higher purpose. In doing so, you continue the cycle of planting seeds and harvesting abundance—not only for yourself but for others as well.

The Joy of Harvesting Abundance

Harvesting abundance is the culmination of years of hard work, discipline, and faith. It is the moment when the seeds of wealth you planted through ideas, habits, and consistent actions bear fruit. As you reap the rewards of your financial success, take time to celebrate, enjoy the fruits of your labor, and reflect on the journey that brought you here.

However, the harvest is not the end of the journey. True financial success lies in the ability to reinvest, diversify, and continue planting seeds for future abundance. By reinvesting your wealth, sharing it with others, and expanding your financial portfolio, you ensure that the cycle of growth continues for years to come.

Remember the wisdom of Galatians 6:9: "Let us not become weary in doing good, for at the proper time we will reap a harvest if we do not give up." Your diligence, persistence, and commitment to your financial goals will lead to lasting abundance, and with each harvest, new opportunities for growth and prosperity will arise. Embrace the joy of harvesting abundance, and continue planting the seeds of future wealth for yourself and others.

CHAPTER 10

THE LEGACY OF WEALTH

Building Generational Wealth

True financial success extends beyond individual accomplishments. The ultimate goal of wealth creation is not merely to provide for yourself but to build a lasting legacy that benefits future generations. Generational wealth is about passing down not only financial assets but also the wisdom, principles, and mindset required to sustain and grow that wealth. In this chapter, we will explore how to build generational wealth, pass on the mindset of abundance, and teach future generations the importance of financial literacy.

Passing Down the Wisdom and Mindset of Wealth to Future Generations

Financial assets can be inherited, but without the proper mindset and understanding, that wealth may quickly disappear. To ensure that future generations benefit from the wealth you've built, it's essential to pass down the principles that contributed to your financial success. This includes not just the "how" of wealth creation but the "why"—the values and habits that sustain financial growth.

1. Instill a Mindset of Responsibility and Stewardship

One of the most important aspects of building generational wealth is teaching the next generation the value of responsibility and stewardship. Wealth, when managed with wisdom, can grow and benefit many; however, without a sense of responsibility, it can easily be wasted. Teach your children or heirs to view wealth as a tool for building a stable future and as a resource to help others, rather than as a means for extravagant spending.

Proverbs 13:22 says, "A good person leaves an inheritance for their children's children, but a sinner's wealth is stored up for the righteous." This verse highlights the long-term impact of responsible financial stewardship. Passing on the mindset that wealth should be managed wisely and used to create opportunities for future generations ensures that the legacy you build will endure.

2. Teach the Value of Hard Work and Discipline

Wealth that is simply handed down without the principles of hard work and discipline may not last long. It's essential to teach future generations that financial success comes from consistent effort, disciplined saving, and wise investing. Encourage them to understand the value of hard work, not just in acquiring wealth but in preserving and growing it.

Proverbs 10:4 reminds us, "Lazy hands make for poverty, but diligent hands bring wealth." Instilling the value of diligence and discipline ensures that future generations do not take wealth for granted but work to maintain and build upon the financial foundation you've created.

3. Encourage an Abundance Mentality

Passing down an abundance mindset is key to ensuring that future generations continue to thrive financially. Encourage them to view wealth not as a finite resource but as something that can grow and expand with the right mindset and actions. Teach them to look for opportunities for growth and to approach challenges with optimism and creativity.

Philippians 4:19 reminds us of God's provision: "And my God will meet all your needs according to the riches of his glory in Christ Jesus." By fostering a belief in abundance, you empower future generations to seek out opportunities, take calculated risks, and build on the wealth they inherit.

The Importance of Teaching Financial Literacy

Building generational wealth is not only about passing down assets but also about teaching the knowledge and skills necessary to manage and grow those assets. Financial literacy is the foundation of responsible wealth management, and it's crucial that future generations are equipped with the tools they need to make informed decisions.

1.   Start Early with Financial Education

One of the best ways to ensure that future generations are financially literate is to start teaching financial principles early in life. This can begin with simple lessons about saving, budgeting, and the value of money. As children grow older, introduce more complex concepts like investing, compound interest, and financial planning.

Proverbs 22:6 encourages us to train children from a young age: "Start children off on the way they should go, and even when they are old they will not turn from it." By starting early, you help children develop healthy financial habits that will serve them throughout their lives. Financial literacy is a lifelong skill that, when taught early, sets a strong foundation for future success.

2. Teach the Basics of Money Management

At the core of financial literacy is the ability to manage money wisely. This includes understanding how to budget, save, and spend responsibly. Encourage future generations to create and stick to a budget, prioritize saving a portion of their income, and avoid unnecessary debt. These basic money management skills are essential for long-term financial stability.

Proverbs 21:20 offers valuable wisdom on managing resources: "The wise store up choice food and olive oil, but fools gulp theirs down." Teaching the importance of storing up resources—whether through savings or investments—ensures that future generations can handle financial challenges and opportunities with confidence.

3. Teach the Principles of Investing

Beyond managing day-to-day finances, it's important to teach the next generation how to grow wealth through investing. This includes understanding the basics of the stock market, real estate, and other investment opportunities. The earlier they learn about the power of compound interest and the potential for wealth growth through investing, the more equipped they will be to build on the legacy you leave behind.

Ecclesiastes 11:2 encourages diversification in investments: "Invest in seven ventures, yes, in eight; you do not know what disaster may come upon the land." Teaching future generations the importance of diversification and strategic investing ensures that they are prepared to manage risk and grow wealth in various economic climates.

4. Encourage Generosity and Giving

Financial literacy isn't just about accumulating wealth; it's also about using wealth for a greater purpose. Encourage future generations to adopt a mindset of generosity and giving. Teach them the value of tithing, charitable donations, and supporting causes that matter to them. By instilling a sense of purpose in their wealth, you help them understand that financial success is not just for personal gain but for the betterment of others.

2 Corinthians 9:7 reminds us, "Each of you should give what you have decided in your heart to give, not reluctantly or under compulsion, for God loves a cheerful giver." By fostering a spirit of generosity, you ensure that the legacy of wealth you leave behind has a positive impact on both your family and the wider community.

Creating a Lasting Financial Legacy

The legacy of wealth is more than just the transfer of financial assets; it is the transfer of values, wisdom, and a mindset that ensures continued success for future generations. By instilling the principles of responsibility, hard work, and financial literacy, you equip future generations with the tools they need to not only preserve but grow the wealth they inherit.

As you build your financial legacy, remember the wisdom of Proverbs 13:22: "A good person leaves an inheritance for their children's children." Your efforts to build and pass down wealth have the potential to impact not only your immediate family but generations to come. By teaching financial literacy, instilling a mindset of abundance, and fostering a spirit of generosity, you ensure that your financial legacy will continue to thrive and bless future generations.

With each lesson you impart, you plant seeds of wisdom that will grow and bear fruit for years to come, creating a lasting impact that extends far beyond financial gain. The legacy of wealth is not just about money—it's about equipping future generations with the knowledge, values, and principles that will enable them to carry on the work you began.

Creating a Lasting Impact

Using Your Wealth to Make a Positive Difference in the World

Wealth, when viewed from a holistic perspective, is not solely about personal financial gain or security. True wealth encompasses the ability to use resources for a higher purpose, making a lasting impact in the lives of others and in the world. Once you've achieved financial success, the next step is understanding how to use that wealth to create meaningful change. This chapter explores how to use your wealth to make a positive difference and the spiritual and social responsibilities that come with financial abundance.

The Spiritual and Social Responsibility of Wealth

Wealth brings with it a responsibility that extends beyond personal use. Whether it's through giving to those in need, supporting causes you believe in, or investing in your community, wealth provides an opportunity to be a force for good. From a spiritual perspective, wealth is not just for self-indulgence—it is a gift from God that can be used to bless others and advance higher purposes.

1. Recognizing the Source of Your Wealth

The first step in understanding the responsibility of wealth is recognizing that it is ultimately a gift from God. While hard work, discipline, and wise decisions contribute to financial success, it is God who provides the ability and opportunities to create wealth. Acknowledging this ensures that wealth is used humbly and purposefully.

Deuteronomy 8:18 says, "But remember the LORD your God, for it is he who gives you the ability to produce wealth." Recognizing God as the source of your wealth encourages a mindset of stewardship rather than ownership. As stewards of the resources we've been given, we have a responsibility to manage them wisely and use them to bring about positive change in the world.

2. Fulfilling Your Social Responsibility

With great wealth comes the opportunity to positively influence society. Wealth can be a powerful tool for addressing social inequalities, improving communities, and creating opportunities for those less fortunate. Whether through philanthropy, supporting education, or investing in sustainable initiatives, wealth can be leveraged to make a lasting impact.

1 Timothy 6:17-19 provides clear guidance on the social responsibility of wealth: "Command those who are rich in this present world not to be arrogant nor to put their hope in wealth, which is so uncertain, but to put their hope in God, who richly provides us with everything for our enjoyment. Command them to do good, to be rich in good deeds, and to be generous and willing to share. In this way they will lay up treasure for themselves as a firm foundation for the coming age, so that they may take hold of the life that is truly life." This passage highlights the importance of using wealth for good, not just for personal gain, but as a way to enrich the lives of others.

3. Embracing the Principle of Generosity

Generosity is one of the most powerful ways to use wealth to make a lasting impact. By giving freely to those in need, supporting charitable organizations, and helping others achieve financial stability, you contribute to a world that is more equitable and compassionate. Generosity also has a spiritual component—it reflects the heart of God, who is the ultimate giver.

Luke 6:38 says, "Give, and it will be given to you. A good measure, pressed down, shaken together and running over, will be poured into your lap. For with the measure you use, it will be measured to you." This principle of generosity suggests that by giving to others, you create a cycle of abundance that not only blesses those you help but also brings blessings back into your life. It's through this lens of giving that wealth transforms from a tool for personal fulfillment into a means for broader social impact.

4. Supporting Causes That Align with Your Values

One of the most meaningful ways to create a lasting impact with your wealth is by supporting causes that reflect your values. Whether it's fighting poverty, advocating for environmental sustainability, improving healthcare, or advancing education, aligning your financial resources with causes you care about allows you to use wealth for a higher purpose.

Proverbs 19:17 reminds us of the value of helping those in need: "Whoever is kind to the poor lends to the

LORD, and he will reward them for what they have done." Supporting charitable causes not only addresses pressing societal needs but also aligns your financial success with God's call to care for the marginalized and disadvantaged.

How to Make a Lasting Impact with Your Wealth

Once you've committed to using your wealth to make a positive difference, the next step is determining how to do so effectively. Creating a lasting impact requires intentionality, strategic planning, and a heart for service.

1. Create a Giving Plan

Just as you create financial plans for saving, investing, and managing your wealth, it's important to develop a giving plan that aligns with your values and financial goals. A giving plan allows you to identify causes and organizations you want to support, set aside resources for charitable donations, and determine the level of involvement you want to have in those efforts.

2 Corinthians 9:7 encourages intentional giving: "Each of you should give what you have decided in your heart to give, not reluctantly or under compulsion, for God loves a cheerful giver." By developing a clear plan, you can give generously and joyfully, knowing that your resources are being used to further causes that are close to your heart.

2. Invest in Long-Term Solutions

Creating a lasting impact with your wealth often involves thinking beyond immediate needs and investing in long-term solutions. This could include funding educational scholarships, supporting entrepreneurship in underserved communities, or contributing to initiatives that promote sustainable development. By focusing on long-term solutions, you create opportunities for lasting change that go beyond temporary assistance.

Proverbs 11:25 says, "A generous person will prosper; whoever refreshes others will be refreshed." Investing in long-term solutions not only refreshes and uplifts those who benefit from your giving, but it also brings a sense of fulfillment and purpose to your financial journey.

3. Mentor and Empower Others

Another way to use your wealth to create lasting change is by mentoring and empowering others. This can involve sharing your financial knowledge, offering business guidance, or providing resources to help others build their own financial success. By teaching others how to manage money wisely, you create a ripple effect that extends far beyond your individual contributions.

Proverbs 27:17 says, "As iron sharpens iron, so one person sharpens another." Mentoring others in financial literacy and wealth-building equips them to take control of their financial future, ensuring that the impact of your wealth reaches future generations.

4. Establish a Legacy of Giving

One of the most profound ways to make a lasting impact is to establish a legacy of giving within your family or community. By encouraging future generations to embrace the value of generosity, you ensure that your wealth continues to make a positive difference long after you're gone. This can be done through family foundations, endowments, or simply passing down the principle of giving to your children and heirs.

Acts 20:35 reminds us of the joy in giving: "It is more blessed to give than to receive." Creating a legacy of giving ensures that the blessings of wealth are shared with others, fostering a spirit of generosity that transcends generations.

Wealth as a Tool for Positive Change

Wealth is a powerful tool that, when used wisely, can create a lasting impact on individuals, communities, and the world. By embracing the spiritual and social responsibility of wealth, you can transform financial success into a vehicle for meaningful change. Whether through generosity, supporting causes aligned with your values, mentoring others, or investing in long-term solutions, the legacy you build with your wealth extends far beyond material gains.

As you use your wealth to make a positive difference, remember the words of Matthew 6:19-20: "Do not store up for yourselves treasures on earth, where moths and vermin destroy, and where thieves break in and steal. But store up for yourselves treasures in heaven, where moths and vermin do not destroy, and where thieves do not break in and steal." True wealth is measured not only in what you accumulate but in the lives you impact and the legacy you leave behind.

By creating a lasting impact with your wealth, you ensure that your financial success is not just a personal achievement but a source of blessing and transformation for others. This is the true measure of wealth—using what you've been given to bring about a better, more compassionate, and equitable world.

CONCLUSION

THE JOURNEY TO WEALTH

Recap of the Principles Discussed

The journey to wealth is not merely a destination marked by financial success; it's a process of growth, learning, discipline, and purposeful action. Throughout this book, we've explored the foundational principles that lead to financial abundance, with a focus on the spiritual, mental, and practical steps that build lasting wealth. Let's take a moment to recap the key ideas we've covered:

1. Wealth Begins in the Mind

The journey to wealth starts with the seed of an idea planted in your mind. Cultivating a wealthy mindset—shifting from scarcity to abundance, visualizing success, and believing in your ability to create wealth—is essential for achieving financial goals. Your thoughts shape your reality, and by nurturing a mindset of growth and possibility, you set the foundation for future prosperity.

2. The Power of Small Steps

Wealth is not built overnight; it's the result of consistent, small actions taken over time. Whether through saving, investing, or paying off debt, each small step contributes to long-term financial growth. Developing daily habits that promote wealth, such as tracking spending, budgeting, and regularly investing, lays the groundwork for financial success.

3. Faith and Action

Faith without action is incomplete. While it's important to have faith in your financial goals and in your ability to achieve them, success requires action. Moving from thought to action—whether by starting a new business, making investments, or taking steps to improve financial literacy—is key to turning ideas into reality.

4. Overcoming Obstacles

Financial setbacks are inevitable, but they are not insurmountable. By adopting a growth mindset, learning from failures, and persevering through challenges, you can turn obstacles into opportunities. The journey to wealth requires resilience and adaptability, knowing that each setback is a stepping stone toward future success.

5. Creating a Lasting Impact

Wealth is not just about personal gain—it is an opportunity to create lasting change. Whether by building generational wealth, mentoring others, or giving generously to causes you care about, wealth can be used as a tool to bless others and make a meaningful difference in the world. True financial success is about leaving a legacy that extends beyond material possessions and impacts lives for the better.

Encouragement to Begin the Journey to Financial Abundance

As you embark on your own journey to wealth, remember that every great achievement begins with a single step. No matter where you are starting from, the principles you've learned in this book can guide you toward a future of financial abundance and fulfillment. The path to wealth is not reserved for a select few; it is open to anyone willing to cultivate the right mindset, take consistent action, and persevere through challenges.

Proverbs 16:3 reminds us: "Commit to the Lord whatever you do, and He will establish your plans." Trust that as you take the necessary steps to build wealth, you are not alone. With faith, hard work, and discipline, you can achieve financial success and create a lasting legacy for yourself, your family, and your community.

Start today. Begin by planting the seed of wealth in your mind, nurturing it with positive actions, and staying committed to the process. Each small step you take moves you closer to your financial goals. Whether it's saving a small amount, learning a new financial skill, or investing in your future, these steps will add up to big results over time.

Remember that the journey to wealth is not just about money—it's about creating a life of purpose, generosity, and abundance. Wealth, when aligned with your values and used for good, can be a force for positive change. By embracing the principles of wisdom, faith, and responsibility, you will not only achieve financial success but also make a lasting impact on the world around you.

So, take the first step today. Your journey to financial abundance has already begun, and with each new day, you have the opportunity to grow, thrive, and build the future you envision.

FINAL THOUGHTS

MONEY AS TOOL FOR FREEDOM AND EMPOWERMENT

Final Thoughts: Money as a Tool for Freedom and Empowerment

Money, when used wisely, is more than just a means of acquiring material goods or achieving personal comfort. It is a powerful tool for freedom, empowerment, and creating opportunities. Financial freedom gives you the ability to live life on your own terms—free from the burdens of debt, financial insecurity, and worry about the future. It empowers you to pursue your dreams, support your family, give to causes that matter, and create lasting change in the world.

At its core, money is a tool that reflects the values and mindset of the person who wields it. For those who approach wealth with responsibility, purpose, and a spirit of generosity, money becomes a force for good, providing not just personal freedom but also the capacity to uplift others. Proverbs 11:24-25 teaches, "One person gives freely, yet gains even more; another withholds unduly, but comes to poverty. A generous person will prosper; whoever refreshes others will be refreshed." In this sense, true wealth lies in how you use your financial resources to empower yourself and those around you.

The Continuous Cycle of Thought, Action, and Wealth Creation

The process of wealth creation is not linear; it is a continuous cycle of thought, action, and growth. It begins with the seed of an idea—your belief in the possibility of financial success. That seed is nurtured through consistent, positive action. Each step you take toward your financial goals, no matter how small, builds momentum. Over time, these actions compound, leading to growth in both financial resources and personal empowerment.

However, the cycle doesn't end with success. Once wealth is created, it must be managed, reinvested, and used for meaningful purposes. The lessons learned along the journey, such as the importance of discipline, perseverance, and generosity, continue to guide your actions as you move forward. The mindset of abundance you cultivate is the foundation for ongoing success, allowing you to recognize new opportunities and continue growing your wealth.

This cycle—thought, action, and wealth creation—repeats itself, not just for the benefit of one person but for future generations. By passing down financial wisdom and principles, you ensure that the cycle continues, empowering others to build on the foundation you've laid.

Embracing Wealth as a Journey

Wealth is not a destination, but a journey that continuously evolves. It requires a balance of faith, disciplined action, and a clear understanding of its purpose. As you embrace wealth creation, remember that money is not the goal in itself—it is a tool that allows you to live a life of freedom, make empowered decisions, and impact the world in positive ways.

As you move forward in your financial journey, remain committed to the cycle of thought, action, and growth. Stay open to learning, take consistent steps toward your goals, and use your resources to create a lasting impact. By doing so, you not only build wealth but also create a legacy of empowerment and abundance that extends far beyond personal financial success.

Proverbs 3:9-10 encourages us: "Honor the LORD with your wealth, with the firstfruits of all your crops; then your barns will be filled to overflowing, and your vats will brim over with new wine." When wealth is used wisely and aligned with higher purposes, it brings both personal fulfillment and the joy of contributing to something greater than yourself. Embrace this journey, and may it lead to both financial success and a life of lasting significance.

www.ingramcontent.com/pod-product-compliance
Lightning Source LLC
Chambersburg PA
CBHW071953150726
47999CB00001B/428